WHEEL
OF SEASONS

RICK MARSI

WHEEL
OF SEASONS

illustrated by
Jan Marsi

foreword by
David Rossie

BUFFLEHEAD BOOKS & PRINTS
Binghamton, New York 13903

Library of Congress Catalog Card Number: 87-90736

ISBN: 0-9619384-1-2

Grateful acknowledgment is made to the Binghamton Press & Sun-Bulletin, and to David J. Mack, Publisher. This selection of columns first appeared there in the same or slightly altered form between 1980 and 1986. Many of the illustrations accompanied the first publication as well.

FIRST EDITION – December 1987
SECOND PRINTING – June 1988

Designed by Jan Marsi

Published by
BUFFLEHEAD BOOKS & PRINTS
P.O. Box 82, Southview Station
Binghamton, New York 13903

Printed at Bell Offset, Inc.
Vestal, New York 13850

FOREWORD

Anyone who can make you enjoy a swamp, it seems to me, is worth listening to and worth reading.

For most of my life I had made it a point to avoid swamps, or having failed to avoid them, to get the hell out of them as fast as I could.

In swamps I have been clutched at by quicksand, beset by clouds of ravenous mosquitoes, and threatened by proprietorial snakes who seemed to sense that I did not belong among them, a position with which I concurred.

Then, one early April afternoon a few years ago, I accompanied Rick Marsi to a section of the Whitney Point Reservoir park north of Binghamton where he said we might observe the passage of some northering waterfowl and perhaps a migrating woodcock or two.

Rick led me along a path for a ways and then moved into heavier cover. As we went, he pointed out new growth emerging in the spring earth and identified some of the many sounds coming from land and water.

I'd seen those plants before and I'd heard the sounds, but they'd always been background, nothing more. Rick gave them dimensions, identities.

The greatest discovery of all came later when I'd realized that I'd just spent an hour in a swamp and loved it.

That is part of Rick Marsi's gift. You can learn from him and the learning is not only painless, it's pleasurable. He is instructive, entertaining, and often challenging, and you can't ask more than that of a writer.

Readers of Rick's newspaper column already know that. Readers meeting him for the first time in these pages will soon discover it.

Not everyone is lucky enough to accompany him on some of his outings, as I've been able to do, but these vicarious nature walks are the next best thing. All you need do is turn the pages and give yourself up to Rick's prose and the splendid drawings supplied by his wife, Jan.

You won't get wet feet or mosquito bites, but that's about all you won't get.

David Rossie

CONTENTS

PART ONE: THE WHEEL

PART TWO: OTHER PLACES

PART THREE: OTHER FRIENDS

PART ONE
THE WHEEL

JANUARY

THE DOG, THE STARS, THE PRESIDENT

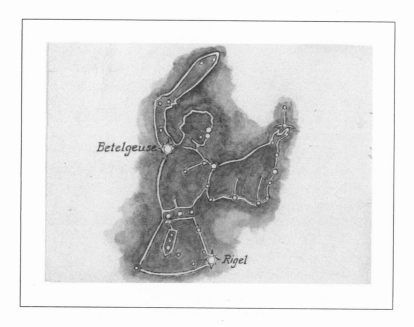

When was the last time the President woke up on a January night and had to let the dog out? It's probably been years, and more's the pity, because the poor guy is missing out on some great astronomy.

I had such an opportunity not long ago - it was garbage night, a Thursday - and came away deeply enriched.

It all started when a dog nose appeared on the pillow and nudged with obvious insistence. These nudges, I have learned through years of trial and error, mean, 'Let me out. I am plagued by gastrointestinal irregularity.'

My usual response is to bolt upright, make with great haste for the front door and facilitate in any way possible this canine flight to freedom. On garbage nights, however, the routine is fraught with added responsibility. On these occasions, I, too, must venture outside, there to serve as chaperone.

For the wind on garbage night is laced with tempting innuendo. Pork chop bones from up the road, potato skins from down - the siren scent of sin is everywhere. The self restraint of well-intentioned pets melts upon contact.

So outward into darkness I plunged - in pajamas, overcoat and rubber boots - to contemplate what the President was missing. He missed Orion, mostly, and a feeling of relative human insignificance.

Often called the Mighty Hunter, Orion is a constellation of sprawling brilliance, more beautiful than any other in the winter sky. On frigid nights, it beams through the southern heavens with breathtaking clarity.

People who enjoy picturing things say the stars in Orion show him standing with a club raised in one hand and a lion skin shield in the other. They also say his right shoulder is marked by a giant star, Betelgeuse. I would tell you how to pronounce Betelgeuse but am not sure. I tried 'beetle juice' once and wasn't rebuked by a nearby cluster of serious sky watchers, so maybe 'beetle juice' is right.

In addition to possessing a shield and large shoulders, Orion also is reputed to own a star-studded belt and a left ankle dominated by a blue-white star called Rigel. Looking up, I really couldn't catch all this. I just saw dazzling pinheads, beautiful and far away.

After staring at the Mighty Hunter for awhile, thinking about light years, specks of cosmic dust, and other humbling things, I drew an imaginary line from his belt toward the southeastern horizon. There, just over the top of a hill, I found Sirius, the most dazzling of all winter stars.

Blazing away from a distance of eight or nine light years, Sirius is universally known as the 'Dog Star,' a name supposedly derived from its location in the constellation Canis Major, or The Great Dog.

Out there on garbage night, I saw things differently. Watching my own dog sniff the breeze, I pegged Sirius as the patron saint of earthbound canines, lighting their way toward pork chops and potato skins.

Gazing out at this brightest star, absorbing the vastness of its celestial medium, I easily could have lost myself in a sky beyond dimension. I might have, too, had it not been for a tiny window of vulnerability between the bottom of my overcoat and the top of my rubber boots. This single weak link was allowing brutally cold air to infiltrate my defense perimeter and gnaw away at flannel pajamas.

There was a whistle for the dog and a retreat over snow that glowed eerie white. Sirius remained behind, sparkling through the branches of a large Scotch pine.

'That's the only trouble with astronomy in January,' I mumbled, now inside and fumbling with large boots. 'It takes place outdoors, at night, when most people prefer being indoors, gazing at television.'

My last reverie before drifting off was about the President. Do you think he ever goes out late at night and stares up at the winter sky? If he had a dog around the place, he might. Otherwise, probably not.

BLUE WHALE FANTASY

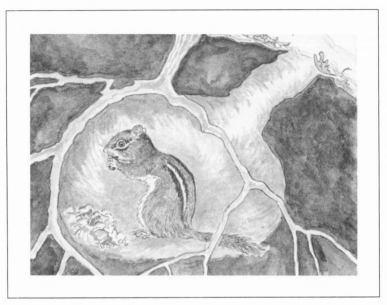

We're all blue whales. Our bodies are encased in eighteen inches of blubber. Even though we're surrounded by icy water, it doesn't cut like steel, doesn't penetrate. When the ocean turns frigid, we swim south. When it warms, we swim north. Our life is always comfortable, a tribute to avoidance of extremes.

Our desire to become one with whales reached its peak on a particular night last week, when a wind of Arctic origin howled around the house, forced snow through seams in the mud room's board and batten, and covered curled-up cats within with white powder. My wife, the kids, me - we looked at each other and felt the simultaneous urge to take on blubber and fin our way toward the world's other hemisphere, which is pointed toward the sun these days and warm.

At that very moment, one of the kids said, 'But, dad, you can't do that. Your boss won't let you. You'll get fired.'

I thought about it. The tyke was right. Perhaps a coping mechanism that allows a person to remain employed while contending with cold weather would be more suitable. After casting aside thoughts of ocean migration, I came up with the following alternative: we would picture other animals that survive the cold and determine how they adapt to winter weather. We would then tailor these successful techniques to our own winter lifestyle.

For example, we all know that cottontail rabbits move from summer nests of grass to more structured quarters, such as brushpiles and hollow stumps, when dropping temperatures tell them it's time. Perhaps we, in turn, should make our own den a tougher nut for winter winds to crack. We'll start by stopping that Arctic blast that seeps in around the door frame. Then we'll put a blanket over the bathroom window, where there isn't a curtain. (A word of explanation: in the country, with only trees and deer around, curtains on bathroom windows are not obligatory. Not having them allows for observation of bluejays, turkeys and other backyard visitors.)

So we'll seal the door and block the window - that should do it for rabbit-like adjustments.

Then we'll move on to adaptations in the mode of garter snakes and lady bugs, creatures that often hibernate in large aggregations. Garter snakes curl up by the dozen below the frost line. Hundreds of lady bugs huddle in masses under loose bark and boards.

Maybe we should try it, this squeezing together business. The whole bunch of us can cuddle in bed. The dog will sleep on our feet.

And while we're talking adaptation, let's not forget gray squirrels and chipmunks, two closely related species whose habits we all should emulate, especially in January. Gray squirrels, for example, tough it out, foraging about for a living during the worst winter weather. Super cold wind, driving snow - you'll see them out there, digging up nuts they've buried or eating the buds of beech or maple trees. Inspired by such stoic example, we promise to get up and go to work every day, earning our own little acorns, even when it snows.

Vows such as these, laden with resolve and predicated on perfect attendance, don't flow from us like honey on a hot spoon. We find it easier to follow the path of eastern chipmunks, those lovable creatures that stock underground dens with seeds and nuts, then lock themselves inside at Thanksgiving and don't come out until spring.

For weeks at a time, the chipmunks snooze away, oblivious to storms that swirl overhead. Occasionally, to break the monotony, they'll awaken, roll over, grab a nut, munch on it, roll back over, and go back to sleep.

The best we can do along these lines is to stock the house with Canadian beer, homemade tomato sauce and novels about swashbuckling sea captains. Upon procurement of such stores, we vow to lock the door, close the curtains and concentrate on chicken cacciatore until pussy willows pop.

'When you can't fight 'em, join 'em.' That's what we always say.

'Meet a chipmunk, and you've met a genius.' We say that, too.

A TUFTED TITMOUSE NEW YEAR

It's January. The year is fresh; state and federal governments have issued tax form greetings. Now is the time to make a list of things you hope will happen during the months to come.

This nature watcher makes a huge list every year and watches only one or two wishes come true. The rest are too outlandish, best catagorized under 'excessive expectation.' He hopes for too much, asks the impossible.

I could simplify my wishes - a little more sunshine, a little less rain - but that wouldn't be fun. Under my current policy of favoring the slightly out-of-reach, I get to fantasize that I'm very powerful, that all my whims will materialize. When they don't, it doesn't matter. The fun was in the dreaming.

Try it yourself. Think about the outdoors and all the wonderful things you'd like to see happen in it this year. For starters, throw in some modest wishes; then outrageous ones. While you're thinking these up, you'll see them in your mind. They'll be real.

A sample wish list for the new year is offered below as inspiration. It is topped by several wishes about weather. The first is that road slush be banished from the land. That means no more fenders rotting; no more wipers flapping vainly to combat slop from passing trucks. The second deals with snow. It should stay white after it falls. It should never turn gray, despoiled by cinders. Skiers should be allowed to wallow in it, then it should disappear on a given day, purity intact.

Bird wishes on the list are myriad. Wouldn't it be nice if there were more prairie for the prairie chicken this coming year; more swamps for the swamp sparrow? Wouldn't it be nice if bluebirds got sick and tired of being booted out of nest holes by starlings and started booting back?

Wouldn't it be inspiring to learn that a band of survivalist ivory-billed woodpeckers had been discovered deep in the Louisiana bayou? The ivory-bills, nearly extinct due to habitat loss, would refuse to come out until the federal government agreed to purchase 10,000 acres of primeval river-bottom forest as a woodpecker wildlife preserve.

This observer also wishes tufted titmice everywhere would decide the world needs more tufted titmice and start producing more. And bobwhite quail: I wish they would stop boycotting my humble, brushy corner of the world and move in for a trial run. They could whistle *Bob-white!* at sundown, the way they do on North Carolina sand dunes. I would applaud quietly and dole out cracked corn.

Two other bird wishes focus on warbler invasions and National Tree Swallow Day. The warblers would be legion, their feathers yellow and bright. They would invade every neighborhood in America, flitting, by the thousands, among backyard shrubs.

That would just about do it for depression. How could anybody be depressed with tiny yellow dynamos flying every which way?

As for tree swallows, it seems only appropriate they be honored by our President (an outdoor kind of guy) for the wonderful job they do zapping mosquitoes and other pestiferous bugs. I can hear it now: '...For without the tree swallow, my fellow Americans, mosquitoes would roam unrestrained...'

Designating every June 10 as National Tree Swallow Day would be a nice gesture; a commemorative stamp also would be nice.

Other wishes range from sublime to less than sublime. On the floral side, every springtime patch of swampy woods should burst with marsh marigold; every rich, moist woodland with jack-in-the-pulpit. Dutch elm disease, chestnut blight and beech bark fungus should take a hike and not come back.

On subjects arboreal, thorn apple thorns within three feet of people's faces should turn round and soft at the ends.

As for mammals, IBM or some other public-minded corporation should hire a prestigious public relations firm to set the record straight on skunks and bats. Skunks eat grubs. Bats eat bugs. They're really decent mammals. Really.

While we're at it, let's wish for a strain of white-tailed deer that doesn't like bib lettuce, carrot tops and other garden fare.

Finally, how about having Ronald Reagan and Mikhail Gorbachev discover they're both batty about birds? They could swap checklists. They could visit one another on census day. 'Love of Titmice Leads to World Peace' - what a great headline for a new year.

CANNONBALL

The longjohns are by Refrigiwear, the parka by Woolrich, the mittens by L.L.Bean. The winter afternoon - a frigid affair of wind and blowing snow that fades the sun to tarnished silver - is pure North Pole.

Above are ash and oak trees, frozen scarecrows swaying stiff and brittle. Their trunks don't creak but make crackling sounds, like bacon in hot fat. Their upper branches scrape and clatter in the fashion of strangers bumping in a crowd, unhappy at being touched.

Below are two rubber boots - huge, clumsy things - that plod and crunch, then turn to follow bird tracks that are an inch apart and meander toward a grove of hemlock trees.

The tracks are half-filled with hard flecks of snow the wind has flung about in hopes of depositing in some crevice or hollow stump. Ten minutes from now there will be nothing, the marks smoothed away like footprints on a beach at high tide.

Follow the tracks while you can. Find a bird with thundering wings. Find a ruffed grouse.

The three-pronged steps make lazy figure eights through a slash of tree stumps and aspen saplings. Loggers have been here and gone, their saws and skidders reweaving an ecological web. Choice red oak has been taken away; perfect grouse habitat left behind.

Follow the tracks, envisioning the bird that made them. It is walking from sapling to sapling, nipping buds that will fuel it against overnight cold. It is listening for sounds that fit poorly with the wind's natural moan; listening for danger.

For there are hawks, owls, and foxes in these woods. They, too, must eat on winter's coldest day. People walk here as well, sometimes quietly with red hats and guns.

Out on a logging road, over to a clump of multiflora rose - the tracks funnel toward food and sheltered pathways. Rubber boots sniff along behind, following visual scent. They stop at the rose tangle but must walk around where a ruffed grouse meandered under and through. They approach the fallen remains of a spindly white oak and hop upon it to follow tracks across a snow-covered balance beam.

They halt at a spot beneath hemlocks where the tracks disappear.

Look up slowly; you'll see a nervous twitch. Watch as a quiet branch explodes in cascading snow. Hear the *thurrr* of stubby wings as a feathered cannonball makes good its escape. Absorb the perfect profile, barreling through bare branches with tail fanned and crest erect.

Is it truly three degrees above zero? Are cold and snow really making life difficult down in Busytown below? Yes, but don't think about it now. Just walk home feeling warm, because the tracks are gone, the bird is gone and everything is quiet but the wind.

FEBRUARY

ICE HOCKEY AND THE PINE GROSBEAK

Ice hockey, by nature, is a game of concentration. One minute you're bearing down on that little black puck, the next you've skated right past it - all because you didn't concentrate.

Lord knows, the game is filled with distractions. Yawning fissures in pond ice promise to send you sprawling on your belly like an otter down a mud slide. Clumps of rinkside cattails tangle skate blades and twist tired ankles. Wives (some of whom are bruising defense persons) batter one's head and body with sharpened hockey sticks.

In the big-time world of farm pond hockey, the rule is set in stone: concentrate or die.

Considering the painful pitfalls that await skating daydreamers, it's a wonder we dared look up from the ice long enough to notice the robin-sized birds that sat in a clump of sumac at the pond edge and watched our roughhouse antics with calm detachment.

As we hooted, hollered and wobbled about, these strangely tame creatures seemed bent on ignoring us. Even our hockey stick clatter failed to arouse them as they hopped about in the sumac, their thick bills buried in fuzzy red fruits.

Who were these aloof strangers? Why hadn't they disappeared into the gray afternoon sky at first glimpse of us? Where was their fear of BB guns, slingshots and the family of man?

We decided to find out.

Walking boldly toward the sumac, we stopped under its gangly branches and stared at the birds from such close range we could hear their soft whistles, intertwined with the crisp snipping of sumac seeds.

Not only had these birds ignored our intrusion, they appeared reluctant to let it ruin their dinner conversation. Looking at their forked tails, heavy bills and the brick-red plumage of a lone male, we recognized these undaunted gourmets as pine grosbeaks. Concurrent with our identification came an immediate understanding of their fearless, tolerant ways. Pine grosbeaks live most of the year in the wilds of Canada, north to the tree line and far from human encounter. There they spend a good deal of time eating tree buds, fruits, and conifer seeds. It's a quiet life, perfectly suited to birds of docile and trusting temperament.

Every once in a while, however, winter food shortages force pine grosbeaks to leave their quiet conifers in small flocks and venture south in search of beechnuts, sumac and mountain ash fruit, and the seeds of spruce, larch, and pine.

Refusing to line up at the feeder tray with their kin, the evening grosbeaks, these gentle visitors often go unnoticed during their rare and unheralded forays into civilization. What a pity. Nowhere in the world of birds is the combination of impressive beauty, tender song, and gentle tolerance of human presence more winsomely exhibited than in the personality of the pine grosbeak.

A century ago the grosbeak's trusting spirit occasionally led to its persecution. Youngsters amused themselves by catching grosbeaks in baited traps made from sieves, propped up by a stick with a string attached. After falling prey to a hand net or slip noose, the birds often were imprisoned as pets. Scientists shot them for study skins; gunners for target practice.

Nowadays trapping and shooting songbirds is illegal; most people wouldn't do it anyway. Having forgiven our past transgressions, the grosbeaks still want to be friends. To this day you can walk up and practically touch them.

Talking quietly and imitating their soft, whistling calls, we watched the flock of pondside grosbeaks until our necks got stiff. They sat and chewed through sumac fuzz, watching us and whistling among themselves.

It wasn't until we resumed skating and banging into each other that they departed with the roller coaster dips that characterize their undulating flight.

We took the timing of their departure as a message to humanity: pine grosbeaks will put up with just about anything - except bad hockey.

A COLD AND BRUTAL SCULPTOR

It is force in a funnel, roaring through downtown corridors, tilting people into leaning towers. It is freedom gone wild, whipping across open fields, numbing faces with a chill that aches to the bone.

It is the wind, called 'Hawk' by people in Chicago, called cold and brutal sculptor by anyone, anywhere, buried in the drift that is dead of winter.

The wind has howled off and on for the past several weeks. It took winter and made it more than winter. It took roads and made them dunes. It took birds, mammals - people - and made them forget about frills.

Sometimes the wind had an ally when it blew, an ally without whom its power would have seemed less complete. There was snow on the ground when the wind came. It was fine and powdery, glinting with rhinestone facets when viewed through car windows on bright Sunday mornings. There was a foot of it - a million flakes shimmering in the sun, waiting to fly again.

When the wind began blowing, it blew at night. It seeped through windows, making hot stoves cold. It brought quilts from closets, longjohns from mothballs. It made people lying in bed hope daylight would come soon.

When daylight did come, roads were without edges. Snow dunes sloped from both sides toward the middle. Highways through flatlands were buried completely as drifts spilled unchallenged from neighboring fields. The leading edge of each drift was topped by snow swirls that hovered above it like sea mist over breakers when the wind is offshore.

Tree bones creaked in woodlands. Pine needles, ripped away, lay scattered on snow. Oaks, ashes, maples had turned to brittle splinters. Human eyes looked upward, waiting for giants to come crashing down.

Birds in the wind faced a cruel paradox. While the cold forced them to search for food, it also threatened to sap more energy than might be gained from morsels found. It was Russian roulette; everyone played.

Seized by a surprise gust, dark-eyed juncos blew about like bits of paper. Tails and wings akimbo, the charcoal snowbirds finally broke away and hunkered in the lee of an outbuilding, pecking at grit and corn. Their breast feathers swirled - first one way, then another.

Bluejays, crests askew, clung to suet baskets spinning wildly. Crows rocketed overhead, heading who-knows-where on a one-way street. Squirrels humped through drifts like stranded seals.

Everyone looked for someone else's path. Skiers looked for snowmobiles; there weren't any. Down went skis through fifteen inches of fluff and mouse tunnels. Thigh muscles strained to resurrect buried slabs. Push-plow-push was the only rhythm.

A single line of turkey tracks appeared and disappeared in the drifts ahead. Crater-shaped bowls told where deer had dug deeply but found little. The world was drifted over.

For people outdoors in a brutal world, there was no pushing on. They retreated, past snowy church steeples tucked deep within pines. They put their backs to the wind, called 'The Hawk' victorious, and let it blow them home.

HUNT NO MORE FOR HIDEAWAYS

Not long ago, I wrote a piece in which I sang the praises of a lakeside hideaway. My natural oasis, I called it, an unblemished world where dragonflies whirred and wood ducks swam circles in the duckweed. Everyone should have a place like this, I wrote, away from drive-up windows and highway noise.

'Go to your own hideaway as soon as possible,' was my advice. A week or so later, I got a letter from a woman who didn't have one to go to.

The woman wrote of how she loved the outdoors and used to camp with her family at every opportunity. Wherever they went, she always was on the lookout for a 'dream spot hideaway' that might be theirs someday.

When her husband died suddenly, those dreams were brought up short. Hideaways were forgotten.

'The kids are grown now,' she wrote. 'I feel lucky to have a comfy chair in the back of my small bungalow where I can enjoy chipmunks, rabbits, and songbirds.'

'You don't need a hideaway,' she concluded. 'You can find it in your own backyard.'

She's right, of course. Why accept only pin-drop silence when the real world groans and squeaks? Why long for the solitude of a virgin forest when a peek out the kitchen window reveals a handy microcosm of survival, success and failure in the wild?

Look, for example, at a band of tree sparrows. Tiny forms scraping for seeds before sundown, they seem too small to survive the winter night that awaits.

Look at the tracks of songbirds, rabbits and cats. They hop randomly, or stalk in silent pursuit. They tell of death and survival, of journeys made and those not completed.

Look at a red squirrel. It flees the bird feeder in a series of lightening-fast leaps, pursued by a dog that takes fewer, but longer, strides and gains ground. As the distance between them narrows, the squirrel's sharp claws carry it to safety in a nearby pine.

Listen to the wind. It blows at night from the northwest, bending trees and pushing them, shaking their branches against a shimmering backdrop of city lights. It still is wild, although siphoned through dozens of cities since leaving its tundra starting place.

Follow a stream that swells in a winter thaw. You'll hear nothing save the rush of water toward unseen rivers.

Take a walk in a snowstorm, where clouds of white shrink the world into nearby shapes and muffled steps. Vanished is a row of adjacent houses, curtained is the view of nearby factory stacks.

Look up at the night sky. Watch Orion's hunter shiver under a quarter moon. The magnitude of this constellation's light-year distance from earth will seem no less awesome to you than to observers in a wilderness.

It's a matter of opening your eyes, of seeing the extraordinary in the commonplace. Wilderness is a state of
mind, unleashed by the imagination, always there when
you want it to be.

MISCHIEF ON WINGS

He's a backyard bully - the noisiest, gaudiest bird in the woods. He's a meddling loudmouth, the one chickadee fanciers love to despise. He's the blue jay, inimitable showoff of the eastern forest.

The bare limbs of winter allow us to watch this engaging rascal in action, filling the woods with a ceaseless barrage of whistles, squeaks, and screams. If we watch closely, perhaps we can figure out why some hail this bird as a lovable clown while others view its antics as those of a scoundrel.

Anyone who feeds birds has an opinion about blue jays. From dawn until dusk their harsh, slurring calls fill the air as they gobble down sunflower seeds and suet. Sparrows disperse in flustered disarray when a gang of jays arrives. As one jay lands on the feeder and gorges, others perch smugly on nearby branches, loudly congratulating themselves for having chased away titmice and finches.

Although appearing to dash about recklessly, blue jays keep track of everything. A house cat slinking about; a snoozing screech owl in a dense pine grove; silent skiers sliding through deep snow - all are spied by blue jay sentinels, then berated so loudly that everyone for miles can share in the find.

Although loud as a rule, blue jays are equally adept at turning secretive and unseen. During spring and summer, the woods and fields seem devoid of jays. No bright blue wings flash through treetops. No telltale songs mark a blue jay presence. The jays have disappeared, absorbed by foliage.

They aren't gone, actually; they're just unperceived. Chances are, blue jays are nesting in an evergreen right next to your house. Throughout the day, with nary a sound, these once-blusterous buffoons slip in and out without being seen.

During such prolonged periods of silence, one can't help wondering what the sneaky jays are up to. Just as the sudden silence of young boys is disconcerting, so is the conspicuous absence of the local bunch of jays. Once either group drops out of sight, you're nervous.

The more public side of the blue jay personality resurfaces with the end of the nesting season. Suddenly, jays are everywhere, hollering for no apparent reason. Listening to their clamorous calls, one often is treated to mimic sounds second only to a mockingbird's.

As is apparent from this brief description, the blue jay is an intriguing mixture of mischief and good-heartedness. Is the gaudy jay a hopeless reprobate, beyond redemption? Or, is it a colorful jester, placed on earth to buoy spirits with antics and raucous calls?

Before you decide, watch out the window as a brash blue joker whirls through gray winter skies. One fact will emerge: a world without blue jays would be dull beyond words.

MARCH

IN PRAISE OF MUDDY INTERLUDES

You might think March is a waste of time - a muddy interlude between what was and what soon will be. It's not really warm, not really cold, this month when seasons change. Skiers rue its arrival. Gardeners bide time until it goes away.

But March deserves to be. It's a time in the middle, between thaw and frozen ground, sleet and warm spring rain. It's a beginning. It is expectation.

Without March, things would come too easily. If you skipped it and went straight from February to April, you'd

awaken one morning and spring would just be there, ready
to heat and serve. Birds would be singing their hearts out.
Lawns would resemble those Florida fairways shown on
TV in January. There would be no transition.

'What's wrong with that?' you might ask.

It's too civilized.

What fun is a season if it doesn't arrive kicking and
screaming? What fun is it if there aren't false starts, re-
lapses, surges forward, glimpses back, and promises finally fulfilled?

Remember how mom and dad always said you had to
work hard for something to enjoy it? March makes you
work. When April comes, March makes it sweeter.

I work out in March along riverbanks and slushy, thawing lakes. I'm looking for waterfowl - canvasback, wood
duck, pintail, merganser. I want assurance these birds have
returned.

They never would have left had things not turned so nasty last fall. But that's the way seasons are when you're a
duck. One minute you're rooting for tubers in a prairie
marsh, the next there's skim ice everywhere. One minute
you're dabbling in the bulrushes, the next their stems have
turned brown and are sinking toward rebirth as muck.

Water has frozen. Food has died or been covered up.
Migration means survival.

The ducks fly south and wait. They haunt bayou swamps,
skim protected bays and ride the ocean when it's calm.
Before long, a new year dawns. Winter months wane; the
sun rides higher. As days slowly lengthen, nuptual plumage
grows iridescent. Ducks find themselves courting, needing
to find North again.

They return in March, when rivers run full and lake ice
cracks and softens.

Six hooded mergansers flash over flooded sycamores. The
river they follow flows chocolate brown, riled by rains that
rip soil from hilltop farms and rush it toward lowland

basins. The birds bank sharply, cup wings, and lose altitude. Dropping through twisted branches, they vanish into backwaters no one sees.

Tree swallows dip by the dozen toward the river surface, snapping up aquatic insects that will feed them until warmer days arrive. Soon will come beetles, flies and butterflies. Swallows on fence posts will feast.

For now, they scrape for what they can get.

Being there watching them, you feel winter about you, not spring. The morning is raw, the sky forboding. Squalls blotch it here and there, ghost-white sheets in a charcoal boudoir.

Your boots leak; your ears are cold. The foolish baseball cap you're wearing should be banished until May. Baseball caps in March are straw houses, and you're the first little pig. You need bricks in March - a wool hat and mittens - to thwart the last wolves of winter.

But why fight the wolf? Isn't there a living room somewhere, and fare on the video screen? There might be, but it won't make you glad you're kicking around for one more spring. Seeing mergansers does that. They're pushing themselves, and so are you. They're not waiting for spring on a platter, and neither are you.

April, when it comes, will be deserved.

THE KEY TO PORCUPINE ROMANCE

Winter's end makes me feel like a porcupine - plodding, listless, sorely unimpressed with the progress of mankind in its search for the perfect civilization.

Porcupines suffer from the same March ennui. They're tired of winter - tired of holing up in the same damp cave every time the weather turns bad; tired of climbing the same old tree to eat the same old bark; tired of always being on the lookout for a great horned owl that may be hungry enough to tempt fate and attack the spiny walls of their quilled fortress.

Sharing the same seasonal malaise, the porcupine and I have worked out a spiritual support system to get us through these trying days. Every year at this time, on a blustery afternoon when the sun is blanketed by clouds of medium gray, I go in search of the noble quill pig. We will commiserate, the porky and I, assuring one another that spring surely will sprout with the following dawn.

It has developed over the years that one of us ends up doing most of the work to make this rendezvous a success. It is not, under normal circumstances, the porcupine.

The porcupine, for example, does not have to climb to the top of a steep, forested ridge and clamber about on rock outcrops looking for caves in the protruding sandstone. The porcupine already is there.

As a matter of fact, the porcupine isn't even required to make a personal appearance. It just has to leave a sign of its presence to let me know it's survived another winter.

This sign takes the form of porcupine scat - hundreds of fecal pellets forming a carpet several inches thick at the cave entrance. That's all I need to know a porcupine is inside his darkened bastion, watching me with listless winter eyes.

Porcupine pellets are an inch or so long and rather neat in appearance. They look like chewed up bark, which is what they are. Bark is all porcupines eat in winter. Sometimes they feed on the same tree for weeks at a time until its outer skin is stripped completely.

This can get mighty boring, compared with the varied fare upon which porcupines dine during more imaginative seasons. Not only are water plants and tender leaves available in warm weather, but canoe paddles, ax handles, and the odd front porch as well.

It's a craving for salt that drives porcupines to chew canoe paddles and porches. The tiniest whiff of the stuff sends them swooning. That's why they hang around the highway and end up getting hit by cars so much - they're after the road salt.

That's also why they're not above gnawing on mufflers and tailpipes. Several years ago, a camping friend awoke to experience this thrill in the middle of the night, in the middle of Alaska. He was sleeping in a Volkswagon bus, the bottom of which featured that particular brand of petrified road slop that makes upstate New York winters so memorable.

Hearing a contented crunching under his bed, my friend investigated. Several porcupines were dining by moonlight on muffler au gratin. They refused to be discouraged until their dinner drove off to another campsite.

About the only thing porcupines enjoy doing more than chewing salt is mating. During the autumn rut, they actually deign to associate with one another instead of waddling about like curmudgeons, ignoring their fellow quill pigs at every turn.

Have you thought much about porcupines mating? Keep in mind that, except for their stomachs and faces, these creatures are covered with quills. It takes the proper mood of cooperation on both sides to bring their rather delicate ballet to fruition.

If the truth be known, everything in porcupine mating hinges on attitude. If porcupines want to mate, they can flatten their quills against their bodies and carry on unhindered. If one of them is unwilling, however, that's the end - no debate.

The autumn mating season also incites porcupines to fits of unbridled song. You can hear them grunting, coughing, mewing, chattering, and shrieking from a quarter mile away when their armor is pierced by the barb of Cupid's quill.

A porcupine's own quills are notably less romantic. With barbs that slant backwards, they work inward when imbedded and can cause a lethal infection.

You'll always know when you've displeased a porcupine, and it's considering hostile action. It will turn around, try to bury its head under a rock, arch its quills, and swing its tail back and forth rapidly. If you get in the way during all this, you're dumber than the porcupine.

Only once have I met a porcupine face to face on my late

winter sojourn to the forested ledge. It had wedged its way, headfirst, into a rock crevice and greeted my approach by fanning the quills on its backside and holding its ground.

That, as I remember, was the moment I decided the porcupine could leave its little pellets at the cave entrance and didn't have to show up in person.

WHEN GEESE AND SKY ARE ONE

When the wind blows warm in March, and freedom from work allows you to stand outdoors feeling it, you figure you're luckier than most. When thousands of Canada geese ride that wind, soaring overhead toward spring, you figure it's more than luck: you've been blessed.

It was a Sunday when the geese came this year, on a morning when people in bathrobes sneaked out for papers and felt zephyrs on their ankles. Farther up the road, higher up the hillside, oak ridgetops blocked a strong southerly breeze and thrust it skyward. Skein after feathered skein soared atop the resulting plume.

The first flock appeared at 10:30 A.M. or so, its conglomerate honk riding fast before it on the wind. I was filing a saw chain in the garage when the sound whipped by. The honks wavered slightly, as their makers would when they crested the steep oak ridge.

Hearing them, I stopped filing the chain, hurried outside, and looked up. Of course I stopped. Of course I looked up. I do it every year. So does everyone else when the first geese fly.

A well-formed wedge of fifty or so birds hurtled over the hilltop half a mile away. I blinked twice, took a breath, and they were overhead, necks outstretched, wings hardly beating.

The earth still functioned; seasons spun. Earth and earthlings had survived another year. These things were instantly confirmed.

More honks wavered, loud and soft on the wind. More geese appeared, then more. For the next two hours a ceaseless stream coursed overhead. Every minute there were birds to see, some close enough to flash white bellies and jet black necks; others on the far horizon, wisps of smoke.

Some of the flocks seemed bent on rigidity. As the wind swirled around them, warping their chevrons, they fought back, closing ranks. Others gave themselves over, letting gusts render their Vs illegible.

Perhaps these geese were headed for a deep blue lake some fifty miles away. Soaring past a gray-sky background, disappearing over a northern horizon just minutes after appearing over a southern one, they would be there within the hour.

They barely had to flap, only balance. The challenge wasn't moving forward but maintaining aerodynamic integrity. The geese did it beautifully. Tipping slightly, cupping wings and straightening them, beating hard, then slowing down, they hurtled through swirls in control.

This was the wind of their dreams - wild, perhaps, but fast and efficient. Old ones knew this from experience. Young ones just knew it.

Several red maples, a black cherry, a sweet birch, and a white ash fell while the geese flew by. They fell heading north, with help from the wind. I would cut for a time, turn off the saw and look up. The geese would be there. I would cut again, look up again. Still more geese.

The cherry, the birch, and the ash were dry, their winter sap still hidden in roots below. Only the maples oozed sweet, clear fluid from severed branches. They thought it was spring already, those maples did. So did I. So did the geese overhead.

BLUEBIRD SUNDAY

We were outside playing baseball, but the weather wasn't right. The sun was bright enough, brilliant, in fact. The grass was dry enough, its puddles all but soaked away. Only the warm (significant) part of the ritual was missing.

We breathed out and saw clouds. We tossed up handfuls of dusty leaves and watched them sail before a stiff west wind.

Then we decided to play softball with gloves on, which, of itself, indicates how confused we were about what season it was. Our cold side said cut wood, wear a down vest. Our warm side begged for baseball.

Sports won. Vernal urges overwhelmed meteorological discretion. Early March, a time famous for gloveless people with cold hands, had done it again. Another early

March, another false start.

Fortunately, there were silver linings. One was watching young boys chase about in a beaten down pasture, bumping into one another, learning bunting, stealing, throwing home. Another was swatting the old cowhide a country mile with a real wooden bat. The best was watching bluebirds.

Their song hit us first, a low-pitched warble floating sweet and soft from a twisted, played-out apple grove. Surrounded by bare fields and silent hedgerows, barely audible over wind and children's voices, the melody struck our ears as incongruous - a vibrant aural painting in a gallery of somber tones.

More incongruous, more stunning, was the singer himself. Bathed in bright sunlight - his tail, back, wings, and head exploding in azure blue - a male bluebird sat among wizened apples, watching the ground.

Alive in the matted stubble were wolf spiders, scuttling about in weak sunlight, slowed but not immobilized by raw winter's end. The bluebird fluttered from his perch, alighted on the ground and snatched them up.

In a nearby hedgerow, perched above a dirt road that freezing and thawing had rendered nearly impassable, a female bluebird added muted accompaniment to the male's sunlit flashings. The wind ruffled her grayish body feathers. Subtle azure shadings washed her wings.

The bluebirds that belonged in this country place were back - always in advance of official spring, always giving notice of winter's final loosening with song and brilliant hue.

In the weeks that followed, the birds would fly in tandem over hedgerows and bobolink fields. The male would sing in flight while both birds scoured the landscape for nest site cavities. Every abandoned woodpecker nest, every orchard knothole would be scrutinized. With luck, a freshly cleaned bluebird house behind the farmhouse also would rate inspection.

Wherever the bluebirds nested, the man and the boys whose farm they now graced were sure the birds would stay through summer. They always did. Things wouldn't be right without them.

'Come on, you're up,' shouted the resident softballers. (Upon sighting the bluebirds, a visitor had become sidetracked - rushing from the batter's box toward binoculars in the car, stalking the male bluebird in awe of color that could be so alive.)

'Come on, let's go. You're up.'

It was easy for them to say. They'll have bluebirds all summer long.

APRIL

SMELLING SKUNK CABBAGE

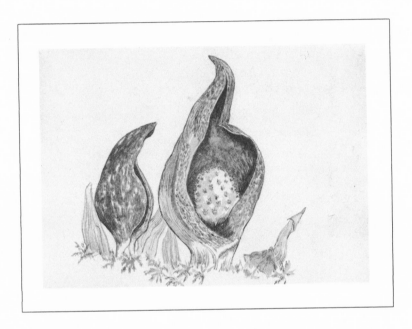

Does it stink or doesn't it? Let's clear the air about skunk cabbage.

We begin by examining the premise that there is no such thing as a bad smell. That which offends the debutante is a carrion fly's delight. It all depends on who's doing the smelling. If you're a honeybee or gnat, the fetid fragrance of skunk cabbage will prove irresistible. You'll defend the attributes of this mucky denizen by arguing that a spate of hearsay has resulted in its odorous and unfounded reputation.

If you're not a honeybee, however, the sap of sweet praise may flow more slowly. Most humans, it seems, would rather picnic downwind from a sewage plant than keep company with skunk cabbage.

'The flowers smell like carrion; the leaves like a skunk,' wrote the late Euell Gibbons of skunk cabbage and its powers. Botanist William Niering was equally under-whelmed: 'Its strong fetid odor resembles decaying flesh,' he wrote in the National Audubon Society's *Field Guide to North American Wildflowers.*

Are things really that bad? Not quite. Bolstered by careful planning and a word or two of caution, the layman can approach skunk cabbage unarmed and unafraid. For those who flare their nostrils in the cabbage patch without proper preparation, however, there awaits pungent purgatory.

A successful visit with skunk cabbage hinges on timing and location. The morning after an early April snowfall is best. Skunk cabbages already will have sprouted, their spike-like spathes sticking out. You'll find them readily in wet woods, along stream banks and in swamps.

Wet snow quiets your step as you walk toward the low spot where skunk cabbage grows every spring. On this particular morning, the swamp is filled with distractions. A male marsh hawk sweeps by, gray and ghostlike over last year's flattened grass. Drake hooded mergansers chase one another through flooded woods, fanning white crests and swelling their necks for a pair of somber hens who demur in nearby shallows. Throughout the sodden forest, in standing water and on spongy bottomland, beds of skunk cabbage are getting a jump on spring.

Each plant has poked its spathe several inches above the ground. The spathe is a leathery hood, resembling cupped hands, that protects small flowers hiding within. The flowers are clustered like tiny burrs on a club-shaped stem called a spadix.

Those skunk cabbages growing on solid ground already have dispensed with last night's dusting of white. Around each plant, a circular hole has been melted in the snow. Skunk cabbage plants generate enough heat during the early stages of blooming to thaw the ground around them and melt their snowy surroundings. They do this by varying the amount of oxygen they consume during respiration. For a two-week period after its flowers are exposed, a skunk cabbage plant can maintain a temperature inside the spathe that is 36 to 63 degrees above that of the outside air. When outside temperatures drop, the plant kicks on an automatic thermostat that increases its use of oxygen to keep things cozy around tender flower parts. On a 45-degree day, you can reach inside a skunk cabbage's leathery hood, and the spadix will feel warm to the touch. To keep heat in, the tissue of the hooded spathe is filled with small, separated air spaces that look like Styrofoam and serve as ideal insulation.

All this heating gives skunk cabbage a head start over other plants in flower and seed production. It also provides a warming area for honeybees who feel obliged to visit the cabbage's pungent heart but are reduced to lethargic flight by air temperatures in the 40s and 50s.

What the bees get for their trouble is pollen and nectar. What the skunk cabbage gets is cross-pollinated. It receives pollen the bees inadvertently have transported from other skunk cabbages they visit during their travels.

The smell skunk cabbages use to attract insects is mild and inoffensive - a smattering of garlic, perhaps, on fettucini alfredo. You can stick your nose right into a spadix and live to tell the tale.

There is another side, however. Only when the plant is bruised or, worse yet, uprooted and taken home, does it unleash an odor unequaled in the annals of chemical warfare.

Why would you want to take a skunk cabbage home? Some folks find it palatable. Euell Gibbons claims if you dry the root for a month, grind it up and mix it with whole wheat flour, you can use it as pancake batter. This man would try anything, keep in mind.

Although eating skunk cabbage may not appeal to the majority, there's bound to be one person out there who will learn the truth firsthand.

After finding a cabbage patch, the wild gourmet will dig up a bunch and toss it in the back of the car. Hardly any smell at all. Can't wait for skunk cabbage pancakes!

Halfway home, with a warm spring sun beating through the window, an ungodly stench will curl around the bucket seats and make this person long for death. Only then will the poor soul realize skunk cabbage and its striped, mammalian namesake are one and the same.

WOODCOCK SERENADE

It's a known fact that naturalists often partake in activities that defy the norms of accepted behavior.

They embarrass themselves in elevators, imitating the mating trill of American toads. They prowl highways for roadkills, hoping to find a porcupine that will complete their collection of rodent skulls. They travel thousands of miles to look at a seagull with pink feet so they can say they've seen it when you haven't.

They also have a hard time convincing observers they're really doing what they're doing. Most policemen will give you the benefit of the doubt, but will they believe you're really listening for owls when they find your car parked on a back road at 4 A.M.? Even when you're accompanied by a grandmother with white hair who smiles alot, it takes a stream of fast talking before they believe you're just wierd, not dangerous.

Strangest of all in the nature clan are bird people. One of their most bizarre rituals - one that always requires a detailed explanation - takes place at this time of year. It occurs in brushy fields at sunset and is called woodcock watching.

Woodcock are strange and beautiful birds, with russet bodies the size of a large lemon, and long bills that suck earthworms from damp soil like so many Hoovers on a lint patrol. The bird books say woodcock are crepuscular, which means they enjoy flying at twilight. That's one reason bird people wait until day's end to seek them out.

The other reason is that in spring the male woodcock chooses twilight to present a multi-media courtship production that includes some of the strangest strutting, singing, and aerial acrobatics this side of a carnival midway.

The activity starts when amorous woodcock males return to the Northeast in early spring after wintering along the Gulf Coast. Without wasting a moment, they locate an abandoned field or hillside pasture that will serve as a singing ground upon which they can woo receptive females.

Shortly after sundown, as dusk fades toward deep blue darkness, each male woodcock sits in a small clearing and starts to peent.

Peenting is not in the dictionary. It is unique to woodcock and involves the production of a nasal blast that sounds like a loud electric buzzer.

After five or six peents, spaced several seconds apart, the lovesick male woodcock takes to the air. It's a ponderous departure, like a giant June bug down a long runway. Wings beating madly, going nowhere fast, the woodcock finally flutters away. His wings twitter as he climbs in ever-narrowing spirals. Soon he is a tiny speck, some 200 feet above the singing ground.

At this point the bird people take action. They know that after a minute or so the male woodcock will begin his downward flight, often landing exactly where he took off. They also know that if they get to the landing pad before he returns, they will witness Act II of his courtship performance at close range.

There is mad confusion as they dash to the takeoff point and jostle for position under thorn apple trees and amidst pine boughs.

Meanwhile, high in the sky, the woodcock's twittering has changed to an outburst of melodious chirps. He is about to plummet earthward with zig-zag abandon.

For more than a century observers listened to the woodcock serenade and weren't sure which part of the bird was doing the twittering and which part the chirping. Were the sounds produced by the wings or the voice?

An imaginative ornithologist put an end to the debate by removing a courting woodcock's three outer wing feathers. When the bird took off and there was no twittering sound, it became apparent the ascending chorus was wing-inspired. The descending chirps remained intact, however, providing proof of their vocal origin.

The male woodcock stops twittering and starts chirping only when he is about to dive for the singing ground below. His chirps continue until he is twenty feet or so above the ground when he pulls out of his death dive and flutters quietly to earth. In the nearby brush, concealed bird people await his next move.

Upon landing, the amorous woodcock stretches out his neck, pulls his head down until his eyes are practically resting on his shoulders and begins to show off. He struts about with lowered wings. He bows. He spreads his tail - all for a lady woodcock who passes judgment from somewhere in the shadows. After parading a minute or

two, he takes to the air in one of many repeat perform-
ances that will last long into darkness.

Crouching in nearby bushes, human observers are overwhelmed. They watch flight after flight, glued to front-
row seats, unable to leave. Throughout the city, dinners
go cold while worried relatives huddle by telephones.
Soon the police will be notified; missing person reports
will be filed.

Somewhere in a brushy field, bird people are watching
black specks in the sky, making up excuses that will
brand them as beyond redemption.

WHAT BIRD WAS THAT?

What is it you see, what flash of recognition pierces your cerebrum, when a bird drops from its perch on a hollow tree, dashes for a thicket and allows only seconds in which to make a positive identification?

If birds have been your consuming interest for years, you will see obvious characteristics that quickly differentiate one species from another; characteristics that, both consciously and with blissful ignorance, you have noted a million times and stored away for just such birdwatching moments of truth.

Dead elm, yellow underwings, white rump, undulating flight - all recorded in a second or two. You have the details you need for a solid identification.

If you're a rookie at the bird-chasing game, however, things won't go quite so smoothly. You'll see the blur of an unfamiliar shape. You'll fumble for binoculars and try to focus fast. You will not succeed.

As fast as it filled, the sky will be empty. Your big chance will have come and gone. Gone for good. Too bad for you, rookie.

'What was that?' you'll demand of the all-knowing mentor who walks beside you, swathed in an aura of understated self-confidence.

'Flicker,' the avian guru will reply with unassailable finality.

'How could you tell?'

'Dead elm, yellow underwings, white rump, undulating flight.'

Humbled, indeed, are the uninformed. You are lowest of the low, a greenhorn in the company of sage and mighty bulls.

'Wow,' you'll think. 'What a great birder. There's no way I could ever get that good.'

Nonsense. Even the world's greatest birders started out calling every gull a 'sea gull,' every owl a 'hoot owl,' and every heron a 'crane.' The only difference between them and you is experience.

You want to know how that guru guy got good? He got good from slogging around in swamps on Sunday instead of eating eggs Benedict and lolling about with *Parade* magazine. He got good from filling his binoculars - over and over - with flitting, soaring, flapping shapes. He got good by being there.

And that's the only way you'll ever get good, kid. So go out there and ask a bunch of stupid questions. Follow the pros around and make a first-rate pest of yourself. Before you know it, you'll be knockin' 'em dead.

A few years from now - I promise - you'll be as good as Roger Tory Peterson. So rapidly will your ornithological star have risen that people will begin nagging you to take them on bird walks and show them how it's done. Ever mindful of your humble beginnings, you will smile upon the neophytes and acquiesce.

Young, eager, hungry for knowledge of all things winged, your adoring throng will request a trip to the river,
where April rains have turned your summer swimming
hole into roiling thick brown soup.

As you approach the river bank, three black shapes will
jump from a backwater of flooded willows, then head for
the trees. One, two, three - they're up quickly and streaking for cover before most of the apprentice birders have
even seen them.

Flooded timber, iridescent blue, square tails, white on
the face, no sound - and they're gone.

'What were they? I couldn't focus in time.' A fresh-
faced lad blurts the truth in rueful tones.

'Three male wood ducks,' you'll reply in a voice that
reflects authority but not a trace of condescension.

'How could you tell?'

'They like flooded timber, their wings show iridescent
blue, they have square tails and a white pattern on the
face,' you'll reply. 'Also, had there been a female in the
bunch, she would have called 'whoo-eek, whoo-eek' as
she flew away.'

See how easy it is? I knew you could do it.

THE BARN OWL MEANS NO HARM

It was an abandoned barn like many others - cracked white paint, rusted weather vane, empty stanchions where cows gave milk but couldn't pay the bills. It was a barn where pigeons ruled by default; there was no competition.

Then, on a warm night in spring, the pigeons felt a presence. The presence screamed a long, drawn-out scream when the sun went down. It flew moth-like through the darkness, breast feathers white as a flounder's belly.

The presence was monkey-faced and real. Pigeons sat on hand-hewn beams above the hay loft and felt their eyes widen. A barn owl - with eyes of its own, like dark brown marbles - had found a broken window at the top of the silo. Where silage once blew through the opening and settled in fermenting heaps below, the owl passed on silent wings.

A ghostly traveler had found new quarters. It would roost in this abandoned barn for the next six months, hunting pigeons and leaving their feathers in downy piles on the silo floor.

'We've got a monkey-faced owl down here,' said a farmer on the phone. He had stepped out on the porch one evening and watched a ghostly shape swoop from the silo and knife through purple sky.

'I'll be down tomorrow,' I said. Then I stayed up in bed reading all there was about barn owls and their nocturnal ways.

I learned they're found in all but the northernmost United States, but never commonly. I confirmed their preference for open country, reading that they roost during the day in old buildings and caves, then hunt by night over fields and flood plains. I verified what I already knew about their prowess as hunters: that barn owls are potent killing machines, with powerful eyes and a keen hearing sense.

Put a barn owl in total darkness, and it will capture mice by hearing alone. Put it in bright sun and it will function perfectly, its highly sensitive retinas protected by a nictitating membrane, or third eyelid.

Put it at the top of a silo, staring down at human intruders, and hope it bears no ill will.

I intruded only briefly, long enough to lie on my back among pigeon feathers and focus a telephoto lens on the opening high above. There, watching me from a support beam just below its window to the outside world, was the first barn owl of my life.

Eerily beautiful; harmless to man; murder on rats - I thought these things looking up. The camera followed orders, making smooth mechanical sounds. The owl looked down at my body on pigeon feathers and didn't move.

Film went from darkness to light and back again. Time was a dimension somewhere else, outside the silo, where people knew nothing of barn owls. Finally, feeling contorted and stiff, I stood up. When I did, the barn owl dipped through its window and was gone in glaring sun.

The farmer relates that it stayed through the summer but never found a mate. One night in late October, the presence left and didn't come back. It hasn't since.

Maybe it flew where you are. Look in abandoned barns, old belfries, darkened caves. Be gentle when you find it. The barn owl means no harm.

MAY

WARBLER APPRECIATION DAY

One friend says they move too fast, are too nervous and never stay in the same place. Another says they're too darned small. Another says nothing; he doesn't know they exist.

They're warblers, a family of songbirds whose members are dainty yet strong, gaudy yet retiring, anonymous yet alluring.

You don't get to know warblers, as you do robins, by simply breathing in and out and keeping your eyes open. They won't be out there picking worms on the lawn, waving goodbye, as you race off for work.

You don't get to know them by going into the woods and not paying attention, either. In my short tenure on this planet, I have watched hundreds of people amble along woodland paths, chatting in blissful ignorance about stock prices and auto sales while dozens of tropically colored warblers fluttered overhead.

The point is that warblers don't come easy. They require work. They must be an addiction.

You needn't, however, become overly addicted until spring. That's when these tiny birds ignite insect-fired boilers and head back to the United States from wintering grounds as far south as the Caribbean and South America.

That's when you've got to be ready.

Hopefully, you've been studying your bird books throughout the winter. Hopefully, you've learned which warblers nest in your area and which ones migrate through. Hopefully, you've got quick reflexes. You'll need them; warblers rarely stop moving.

Incessantly flitting, curling, swooping for food - a warbler's idea of rest during migration differs greatly from that of a human migrant who might flop down, exhausted, at a truckstop motel.

It's not that warblers don't sleep during their stopovers. It's just that, in addition, they must devote a great deal of time to stomach-filling.

A trucker can enter a diner, consume eggs, bacon, sweet roll, and coffee in one fell swoop, and be set for hours. A warbler, on the other hand, has no access to roadside diners; no centralized food dispensary. It must fly from tree to tree in search of caterpillars and flying insects that are small and must be consumed in great numbers before adding up.

All this entails the considerable burning of energy; a caloric conflagration, if you will, that requires more food, which keeps the bird on a gastronomic treadmill. While our trucker simply orders a stack of pancakes and eats, a warbler must live the life of a non-stop dietary nomad.

Although this arrangement has proved inconvenient for the birds, it hasn't for their human admirers. A feeding warbler, the birding populace has learned, often ignores a quiet observer.

The observer, if serious about warbler watching, will be looking through binoculars. The average warbler, after all, measures only four inches or so from tip of tail to tip of bill.

Without binoculars, the naked eye can spot a four-inch bird at thirty yards, but will record little save a nervous, blurry streak. With them, the retina rejoices in a bird that radiates color like a brightly colored butterfly.

Some with black masks, others with orange throats and chestnut sides, the tiny songbirds flit through our world in gorgeous anonymity. Few people ever see them well.

Oh, that for just for one day, warblers might be bigger than they really are; as big as turkeys, perhaps. We would parade them through town so everyone could see how beautiful they are. Then they would turn small again and go back to the woods.

We would call this celebration 'Warbler Appreciation Day.' It would take place every year during the first week of May. All schools, businesses and government agencies would be closed.

MAY AND RIVERS FLOWING

You're alone on a river, deep in a valley with steep wooded sides. There are no people, no cars, no road signs saying, 'Go for the gusto.' There is just you, watching what your eyes choose to see.

They see a world transforming, an ecosystem shedding one seasonal skin for another. Shade by delicate shade, this world grows greener, warmer, more hospitable. Niches are refilled by emigres returning from southern exile. Branches sprout nests. Knotholes bulge with blind baby squirrels.

High overhead, the sky becomes display ground. Two red-tailed hawks ride updrafts, their flight feathers flared, their wings flattened. Swirling on an aerial merry-go-round, they carve slow, lazy circles. There is no panic here, no desperation. These birds have found one another. Soon they will feed downy chicks on voles spied with eyes that peer like telescopes.

But first a bond must be formed. The soaring hawks draw closer, their circles tightening. The male lowers one leg, dangling it straight down. Squeezed within tightly clutched talons is a small rodent: a mouse, or chipmunk, perhaps.

Round and round he circles, dangling his prize. The redtail is assuring his mate of hunting prowess, offering to share in rodents captured from this day forth.

Round and round circles the female, watching, absorbing.

Far below, just above a river bend flowing with plastic smoothness, caddis flies flutter on wings that couldn't soar if they wanted to. Wave upon fluttering wave, they move upstream as one, all acting the same, all following an instinctive insect code that says lay your eggs in water, then die with a calling fulfilled.

Walk this riverbank in sunlight, and watch the caddis drama. As flies dip toward the water, laying eggs, rainbow trout surge upward from lairs under rocks below. They surge up with black spots and pink stripes to slash at protein born of the river itself.

Bordering the riffle where trout rise and gorge, clumps of marsh marigold bloom bright butter yellow. Nearby is the pure color white, unsullied on blooms of shadbush and witch hobble. Oak leaves are just emerging, tiny spear clusters furled within slowly opening buds. Wild rhododendron abound, their trunks as thick as your arm, with flowers free for the looking.

A beaver stick floats by. Chiseled by teeth that chew aspens in the dark, the branch has been plundered of soft green bark. It bobs down the river naked, off-white. Somewhere a beaver grows fat, awaiting twilight.

Intrude a bit on this place. Turn over rocks in the shallows, watch mayfly nymphs cling to them. Gills on nymph abdomens twitch with tiny feathers that draw oxygen from the water. Put the nymphs in a cup filled with water;

they will scamper on the sides like spiders. Soon their skin will split down the back, and they will crawl from it toward a different world. Soon they will rise to the river surface - their newly formed wings quickly hardening - and fly forth to mate and die. Soon; maybe later today.

The sun drops imperceptibly. The tail of a water snake disappears under jumbled stones that soon will lose warmth to the dark. Vultures soar on thermals that rise up a cliff face but are fading with sunset calm. Toads trill in backwater pools. A great blue heron flaps toward some secret spearing ground.

Before long night will come. Bats will arrive, swooping on caddis legions. Owls will hoot, but you won't be here. You're a visitor, after all, an observer. It is your place to find a highway, stow the day's images as memory, and leave the river in peace.

SEEK A LEEK

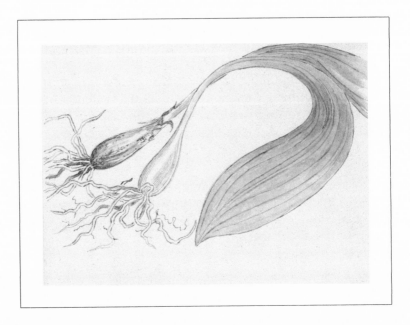

While preceeding the rest of me through a woodland glade one May afternoon, my nose began signaling my brain that I wasn't in the woods at all, but seated in an Italian restaurant.

I closed my eyes, sniffed deeply of an unlikely fragrance that meandered through barely opened tree buds, and played along.

It was late on a Saturday night. The restaurant was one of those cozy neighborhood places, featuring shiny red booths, photos of the owners' parents, and an exhaust fan that caressed pedestrians with a hint of clams marinara.

I was about to order.

'I'll have the eggplant parmigiano,' I said, 'with an order of garlic bread.'

Garlic bread! That was it. That was the smell.

I opened my eyes and scanned the surrounding woodland. A pair of tiny, speckled birds - brown creepers - spiraled about the trunk of an old sugar maple. Their curved bills probed beneath bark fragments, spearing insects that hid from the sun. Wildflowers grew everywhere. Bashful, nodding debutantes, they bowed their heads over rotting remnants of last year's foliage extravaganza. At my feet were clumps of spring beauties. Behind them flowered wood anemone and cut-leaved toothwort, each with fragile white petals that wanted to be noticed but took no offense when they weren't.

There was even a spray of marsh marigold, with brassy yellow blooms that would force you to like butter if you stuck them under your chin.

There was all this - the full spectrum of spring's botanical rainbow - but none of it smelled like garlic.

It was then, at a nadir of sleuthing self-confidence, I noticed a sea of lance-shaped leaves in a streamside clearing.

Each leaf was an inch wide and would bring to bear, if separated from its peers, no major impact on the overall aroma of the surrounding woodland. Together, however, this vegetative conglomerate packed the punch of an olfactory steamroller.

'Leeks!' I exclaimed. 'Mother Nature has lead me to the promised land of good seasonings!'

'Oh, sweet, bulbous herb,' I continued. 'Allow me to remove, with great judiciousness, a portion of your pungent bounty for transferal to my humble kitchen.'

Receiving tacit approval from the waving stems, assuring myself there were more than enough to allow for low-level environmental impact, I whipped a garden trowel from my jacket, dropped to my knees and began extracting a Baggy's worth of leeks.

Wrenching would be a better word. Your average leek, I discovered, is a bona fide trowel bender. Even though it grows in loose ground, its bulb is deeply buried, with far-reaching rootlets that cling to surrounding soil.

With great puffing and grunting I convinced these tendrils I was stronger than they were. The result: my removal of a dozen or so leek bulbs averaging a half-inch in diameter.

After washing them in a chute of stream water that stiffened my knuckles and felt like fifty degrees, I placed the leeks gently in their Baggy and carted them off toward culinary rebirth.

On the way home, whizzing past grayish-green hills that exploded periodically with shadbush blooms, I dreamed of how I would eat my leeks.

A wild onion pie? Chopped leeks and scrambled eggs? Chilled potato-leek soup?

None of these, probably. Leeks taste best when simply simmered until soft in lightly salted water, drained and topped with butter.

Actually, I concluded, it's not so much how you eat leeks that counts, it's what you do after eating them.

What you do afterwards is brush your teeth and your tongue.

That's right. Famous natural food forager Bradford Angier assures leek eaters that breath problems associated with the consumption of leeks are caused by tiny particles that remain in the mouth after eating.

A simple brushing of the teeth and tongue, Angier insists, will remove all fear of offending.

As the essence of leeks swirled about the car and shadbush trees whizzed by, I wondered if the Indian braves who ate leeks from my secret streamed 400 years ago had to worry about offending the lady Indians with whom they shared longhouse bliss.

Definitely not, I decided. I would brush my teeth after eating leeks, but I would not brush my tongue.

OVERDOSING ON DUCKS

It's hard to believe, but Mike used to be an exceptionally well-rounded guy. A little fly fishing, some reading, a Bombay martini or two - his pleasures were those of gentlemen everywhere.

Folks used to marvel at the facile manner with which he could launch into animated discourse on a variety of subjects. The inherent flaw in Le Carre's latest novel; the ethics of an artificial heart; the sharp, yet endearing impertinence of a brand new beaujolais - Mike handled them all with wit and panache.

How drastically things have changed. As I write this, Mike sits alone in his office, avoided by all but his most devoted friends.

No one calls to suggest lunch at the club. No one stops by to discuss thorny philosophical dilemmas. It's sad but true: no one wants to get caught in the same room with

Mike anymore - for fear he'll start talking about ducks.

The tragic transformation started about a year ago, when Mike was convinced by a bird-watching friend to visit a local swamp. The spring duck migration was on, the birder said. There would be good looks at snazzy drakes.

Always eager to explore new paths of enlightenment - unaware it would change his life forever - Mike agreed to the expedition.

Arriving at the swamp pond, the two men gazed out to discover a pair of hooded mergansers resting in the afternoon sun. The male's chestnut flanks glistened. The feathered tips of the female's crest gleamed a pale, delicate cream.

The birder set up his telescope, focused on the courting mergansers and smiled knowingly in Mike's direction. 'Come take a look,' he said, offering the apple to an unsuspecting Adam. 'The male is fanning his crest.'

Peering through the telescope, watching one of the world's most beautiful birds display, poor Mike didn't have a chance.

The drake merganser swam about the female in tight circles, swelling his jet-black neck, expanding his white crest like a Japanese fan, throwing his head back in a series of compulsive jerks. Then, in an explosion of sunlit droplets, he stood on his tail and wildly beat his wings.

Mike gasped. He was hooked forever.

The next day he raced out and bought a $300 telescope; the day after that, a library of field guides. Before long he was disappearing during lunch hours, missing appointments with important heads of state.

Then came the duck letters. 'I went to the swamp yesterday and saw three blue-winged teal dabbling in the duckweed,' he would write to colleagues with whom he had previously conversed on subjects ranging from Middle East tensions to prayer in schools. 'The white crescent on the face was clearly visible.'

'Did I mention in my last letter that the American Ornithological Union has changed the name of the Fulvous Tree Duck to the Fulvous Whistling Duck?' he queried of other correspondents.

No one wrote back.

After that came the duck trips. Upon commandeering the family car, plastering it with bird decals and filling it with muddy boots, tripods, bird books, and binoculars, Mike would leave home on unannounced expeditions. First it was driving 115 miles to buy a paper mobile of flying mallards; then a three week trip to Florida for observations of mottled ducks in their native habitat.

And at home, where the flame of shared ideas and intellectual curiosity often would burn until dawn? Well, the wife hasn't left him yet - that's encouraging. She did threaten to on one occasion, when he began sawing lumber for wood duck boxes in the dining room.

It's all terribly sad.

A month ago Mike began therapy. The doctor told him his only chance lay in moving away from the swampy, marshy Northeast. He starts his job as editor of the *Mohave Tattler* in Dry Crack, California, next week.

Mike, God bless him, is discouraged by his recent misfortune but hopeful just the same. 'If I can just go six months without watching a duck,' he says, 'I'll be able to stay off them for good.'

Out in Dry Crack, his friendly realtor assures him, the temptations will be few and far between.

JUNE

RUN, RABBITS, RUN

The time is late June. Back yards have become perfume crucibles, blending nectar and petal fragrance into scents no day save this one can recreate.

Cottontail rabbits weave through the perfume not knowing if it's June or July. They know only that they are alive, the grass is green and unknown forces bid them nibble it and grow.

Emerging from brushy daytime retreats, the rabbits graze on the lawn at twilight. An evening breeze blows softly, peacefully. Threats of claw and talon are veiled by succulent shoots and clover heads. The world is a daisy chain, stripped of inherent violence by a robin's twilight song. That predators can snap that chain with a pounce or dive is pushed aside for now.

A dog bounds through the daisies and brings their sweet scent home. Young rabbits feed among them and appear vulnerable, much too tame. These cottontails may live until July; they may not.

Still small enough to fit in a pair of cupped palms, the rabbits observe my approach with eyes that glisten quizzically but show no fear. Run, you silly rabbits. Avoid all who come this close. My motives are benign: to inspect your puffy tails; to catch the gleam in your eyes. But what of the next intruder? Will it come on wings that make no sound?

The rabbits munch and watch. I am seven feet away, frozen as they should be when another's movement tugs at peripheral vision. Reacting with an innocence born of youth, they lift their heads, note my presence, then busy themselves nibbling again. The world outside is new. This human may be the first they've ever seen.

Only ten days ago these youths were curled in a fur-lined nest, nursing, growing, knowing nothing of danger. When hunger pangs came, a mother appeared. When a black snake approached, she drove it back with violent kicks from her sharply clawed hind feet.

When the time for weaning arrived, protection disappeared. Not a month old, the young rabbits were out on their own. With luck they would live to see predators walk by them as they lay motionless, letting camouflage work its wonders. They would live to outrun a mink or fox by exploding rocket-fast, then weaving in a zig-zag pattern that couldn't be followed. They would learn every inch of their home range, knowing the location of woodchuck burrows, hollow logs and other sanctuaries that could save them in a chase that meant their lives.

If only they could survive a few more days - a few more weeks - they would learn these things. If only, but the odds weren't good. Thirty-five percent of all cottontails never see their second month of life. Sixty-five percent die before a year has passed.

I dash at the rabbits, waving my arms. They bound for cover, their new legs pounding. Run, rabbits! Learn fear and survive. Live to watch leaves turn red and winter grow cold. Survive to see your second spring.

A FOREST IS FOR WALKING

The forest is dark in June, its duff-covered carpet cool. Departed are early May mornings, when branches stretched like twisted black fingers, grabbing for open sky. Ensconced are days of leafier, more secretive bent, when woodlands become enchanted places, filled with shapes that dart and disappear.

It is now that listeners haunt these glades and read them like open books. Summer forests make hearing an ally, the quiet traveler's most valued sense. Walking, stopping, tuning in, listeners feel no compulsion to see what transpires among darkened boughs above. They can listen, instead, identifying and letting their minds roll motion pictures.

They are freed from binocular slavery; free to hear day

begin.

Dawn, this day, is darkness skulking toward deep ravines. It is music that plays from everywhere but can't be pinned down. The leaves overhead have become a sunrise summer stage; all the performers ventriloquists.

A voice rings out - a loud, whistled, *wheep*, followed by a rolling *preet, preet*. A form darts overhead - robin-sized, with a sulfur belly and tail of cinnamon. It darts by and is gone. The call persists. Motion pictures roll.

Just over there, hidden by waving white ash leaves, a great crested flycatcher is sure to be perched on a dead branch that pokes above the canopy. Forty feet below, in a tree trunk perforated by bark beetles and made domestically suitable by a long-departed family of hairy woodpeckers, is a hole with a three-inch opening.

Inside the tree, six inches below the opening, a nest of grasses, twigs, and a cast off snake skin cradles five creamy eggs streaked with chocolate brown. A female flycatcher warms them, resting in semi-darkness.

Outside, in slanting sun, her mate sits atop his lookout post, awaiting insects ripe for chasing. *Wheep, wheep.* The sound filters down through deciduous foam.

Other sounds waylay it, competing for center stage. Red squirrels *churrr* from hemlock darkness. Chipmunks *chuck, chuck,* then scurry from ferns toward mossy trunks. Dry leaves rustle - a garter snake slips toward self-imposed obscurity. The snake will shed soon. Its skin is pale, with indistinct stripes. Its eyes are glazed, fogbound like the river.

Flickers wheel through unseen corridors, laughing maniacal laughs. Orioles whistle from orchard sunshine beyond the forest edge, admiring a gourd-shaped nest they've just fashioned. Woodpeckers drill, bluejays sound alarms, crows caw, chickadees sing about how being a bird is a very good life.

The eastern sky grows brighter, trading pink for baby blue. A listener stands quietly, seeing little, picturing it all.

WHAT MY NOTEBOOKS TELL ME

On my shelf sit three diaries, testimonials to suns rising daily during three revolutions called years. The oldest testament reads '1975;' the next oldest, '1980.' The most recent is in progress, which means diaries get written around here every fifth year or so.

One night last week, when the house was quiet and the darkness cool, I laid these books side by side on a desk. Opening each to early June, I read of spring in different years.

What struck me was that nature is ever-changing, ever-constant. While wildflower meadows, aspen groves, and other ecosystems can be counted on to grow, mature, and eventually give way to succession, these same plant and animal communities are sure to establish themselves in other places, at other times.

Ten years ago, my oldest diary states, the field next door was awash in devil's paintbrush, an orange flower farmers once considered such a pernicious weed they claimed it came from Satan. Every time the wind blew, this field would awake in a surge of swaying blooms. Black admiral butterflies flitted among them, sipping nectar. Goldfinches ate their seeds.

A decade later, that field and those butterflies are gone. Untouched by humans, the land has matured of its own accord. What were unobtrusive maple and hawthorn saplings now shade the ground, blocking sunlight. For plants such as devil's paintbrush - sun-loving plants of fields, clearings, and roadsides - advancing shade has sounded a gradual, inexorable retreat.

Grieve not, however, for the displaced plant of Satan. No sooner had shade-tolerant species such as wild geraniums and barren strawberries replaced it, than a farm up the road foreclosed, its pasture languished uncut, and new paintbrush habitat was born.

Paintbrushes don't die, they just relocate.

Reading my decade-old diary, I can tell who chose to go with them. Black-eyed Susans vacated, moving their chocolate-brown centers up the road before total shade arrived. Bull thistle disappeared. It curled its vicious spines, assembled the bumblebees that siphon nectar from its purple flowers, and went where a sun-loving plant could still find open space.

Following on the heels of this botanical exodus were birds of the same persuasion. Red-winged blackbirds, song sparrows, and goldfinches all abandoned ship, declaring the field and its darkening confines unsuitable.

Ten years ago, my diary states, all these creatures built nests in my overgrown field. In 1985, my eyes and ears tell me, not one such bird remains.

Should I feel sad, betrayed, abandoned by their

departure? Should I yearn for a sunny paradise lost? I should not, because one set of friends has replaced another. Now partridges lurk where aspens shade the soil. Now an emerging forest grows skyward where farmers planted potatoes a generation ago. Now wood thrushes trill from shaded branches that weren't there when this woodlot was pastureland.

Ever-constant, ever-changing - this my diaries teach me every fifth time the earth skirts the sun.

SLUGS AND SPRING DEPARTING

I was right in the middle of removing a slug from a strawberry when a realization struck: it wasn't spring any more.

Zing! went the slug, rocketing off toward interstellar space. 'Springtime is over,' I thought, as the mucous-laden interloper landed clumsily in a distant patch of rye grass. 'The time has come to remember things I've seen but haven't written about during this young girl of a season that breaks off the relationship before anyone gets too attached.'

And I did.

First I thought of this year's flowering dogwoods and how they exploded in riotous bloom. From urban front yards to lonesome forest glades, every dogwood seemed

to thrive in the damp and cool of an otherwise un-
cooperative May.

I thought of other flowers, too - of the wine-red
rhododendron that made me take its picture fourteen
times; of a scraggly mountain laurel that burst forth so
beautifully as to break the will of my pruning shears; of
white baneberry petals, delicate and clean in the deep
green woods.

And of flowers from the open field? Of ragged robin, Indian paintbrush, and regal crown vetch? I gave each a
fond review, remembering how our dog offers their com-
bined fragrance each time she returns from tall grass
expeditions.

I also thought of bats at sunset and trout streams that
slipped through an awakening countryside. The bats dipped and twisted with a nervousness honed by fast insects
and frenetic genes. Fluttering silhouettes on a deep
orange horizon, they spoke in tones of ultrasonic privacy,
in conversations I wanted to snoop on but couldn't.

Brown trout also awoke in the twilight, rising from
darkened, undercut banks to sip mayflies that wriggled
their newly emerged wings in the surface film. Breaking
above the water for a split second, each trout glowed
honey-brown in the dying light, then rolled and
disappeared.

Then I thought of darkness, and how a quarter moon
played tricks, first cradling Venus in its arms one brief
and beautiful night, then abandoning the white-light
planet to roam unattached in darker portions of a black
velvet playground.

There were other nighttime flashes: firefly signals that
sparkled on country roads; northern lights that sprayed
across the sky in foamy streaks. I remembered them, too.
They made the springtime soft and dreamlike.

There were birds as well, bursting with energy. They
burned the vernal candle at both ends, racing through

four-year lives on an all-or-nothing rampage.

To the following individuals I offered special thanks:

To the male scarlet tanager that paused on a dead branch in bright sunlight to let me soak him in.

To the pair of bank swallows that nested in a stream bank and shared with me my favorite fishing pool.

To the wood thrush that eased me into darkness and softened emerging dawn.

To the house wren that never, ever, shut up, from 4:30 A.M. to 9:15 P.M. and is still going strong.

To the rose-breasted grosbeak that whistled through the ginsing forest and made me feel refreshed.

To all of you: God bless and come again next year. I couldn't have made it without you.

JULY

COUNT THE WAYS TO ENJOY SUMMER

Bird songs don't do a thing for him. Wildflowers are a bore. When pop says, 'Look outside, a cardinal!' he replies, 'How many fingers am I holding up?'

He is three years old and enamored of numbers, a preoccupation that amazes his mathematically crippled progenitors.

'How many toys will fit in my backpack?'

'How many minutes until Sesame Street?'

'How much do I weigh? How much do I weigh when you get on the scale with me? Now you get off slowly and we'll count the numbers backwards.'

Perhaps the nature loving will come with time.

There exist, however, a few tricks that have proven effective in luring the future computer magnate away from magnetic numbers on the refrigerator door. One is the promise of a 'tree chopping' expedition to the great, spooky woods beyond his back yard.

They are slightly on the boisterous side, these tree chopping expeditions. Ruled by the whims of a youthfully indelicate child-monarch, they most grievously violate the forest's primeval silence.

Upon arriving in the woods, the pre-school woodsman immediately finds an ax of Bunyunesque proportions. This he accomplishes by scurrying about the forest floor in search of the perfect dead branch: one that incorporates extreme length, great thickness, and fearsome eye-poking ability.

Once this weapon has been parentally modified to meet minimum safety standards (usually shortened by at least one half, to the accompaniment of great protest squawks), the chopper is afforded ample leeway and allowed to knock his primitive tool against huge red oaks and shaggy hop hornbeams.

And so he rambles, hollering, through the woods, holding pop's hand over insurmountable stones, stopping periodically to 'chop' a tree, trying his best not to step on trillium.

While he rambles about, his father manages a bit of nature watching. It's not easy, mind you. There are the child's vocal exhortations, his numerous tree swats and other distractions. Only by following in the footsteps of countless Hindu yogis is the elder Marsi able to forget the bed of nails, so to speak, and concentrate on a good night's sleep.

There are northern orioles in the trees. They land atop the tallest red maples, scold in tell-tale blackbird fashion, then curl about branches, spearing larval tidbits.

Rose-breasted grosbeaks court here as well, she demurring in streaky shades of brown and tan, he a whistling fool, bedecked in black and white. Sometimes they sneak to the thistle seed feeder, nibbling tiny black seeds, squeaking metallically to one another with obvious understanding.

Also courting are ovenbirds, hopping on pinkish legs from the forest floor to a white pine's lowermost branch. Their tails bob nervously. Orange crowns stand erect.

'Chip...chip...chip.' A warning. 'Chip...chip...chip.'

'A nest lurks on the ground near here,' the woodland warbler proclaims, 'an oven-like tunnel hiding embryonic seeds of future forest songs. Time to watch your step. Time to move along.'

The cherubic woodsman has no objection to changing course. Gastronomic grumblings tell him it's almost cookie time. Better head back to the kitchen and count cookies.

A yellow-billed cuckoo clucks in the thorn apple as we approach the house. 'Two peanut butter cookies and two sugar cookies make how many?' he asks.

Perhaps the nature loving will come with time.

RUFFED GROUSE RUNAWAY

Ponder for a moment the parallels between human nature and the nature we look for outdoors. They are everywhere. One can hardly lift binoculars without watching an animal do something that humans do in a similar fashion.

An example: animals, as we've all been told, have basic needs. They are blessed with an ignorance of fashion trends and of what other animals think of them should they spill their food while eating. These creatures spend most of their time worrying about finding a decent place to stay and getting enough to eat. So do people, basically.

Another example: animals don't like other animals trespassing on their turf and making passes at their mates. People don't either. Animals often bare their fangs to scare these trespassers away; people call the cops or hire a private eye to dig up dirt that will convince the interloper to plow in different pastures.

And, finally, animals are devoted to their young. They are devoted but sometimes show exasperation with little ones that can drive them up a wall. Human parents struggle with these same paradoxical emotions.

In examining this parent/child parallel, we discover that almost all humans view parenthood with great seriousness. They protect their offspring at all costs, nurturing them while in the nest, encouraging them toward independence that lies beyond. Their children becoming focal points, parents orbit about them like caring satellites.

This happens in nature as well. It happened recently on a dirt road that was winding through dappled sunlight when a car and a grouse stopped on it to stare at each other.

The grouse, a female, was alert. Crossing from one side of the road to the other, crest slightly erect, she seemed preoccupied, almost unconcerned that a car had stopped and its occupants were gawking at her like fans glimpsing superstars.

Then came clucks from the grouse, the clue to her mystery. Soft, almost cooing, they were aimed at wayward young. There was a movement, a blur of rust-colored fluff that scurried across the road under the female's nervous gaze. There was another blur, and another.

The grouse chicks looked about two weeks old, pale brown with cinnamon heads. Already good runners, they were limited fliers, flapping with labored wingbeats and not very far. As such they were vulnerable - perfect prey for a goshawk or fox. Their mother knew this and called her brood across the road with obvious urgency.

One by one they crossed, eight in all, while the caring

satellite scurried about them, clucking and cooing, stretching her neck, keeping an eye on the car to make sure it didn't attack. It didn't. It just sat in the woods, engine off, watching her complete an offspring roundup.

Making the mother's work infinitely more difficult was a single chick, a loner with second thoughts. Perched five feet up in a roadside sapling, now all alone on the wrong side of the road, the youngster balked at the big move. Afraid to cross, yet fearing abandonment, it sat on its perch and peeped.

The mother grouse ran from the right side of the road, where the good babies were, to its exact middle. From there she cooed and clucked, even mewed a few times to lure her final chick toward the fold. It didn't work. The young grouse peeped but wouldn't budge.

The hen was in a bind. The longer she left her eight obedient chicks unattended, the farther afield they might stray. The longer she allowed her reluctant baby to play hard-to-get, the longer the entire grouse family called attention to itself in a world where predators pray for standouts.

On stiff legs, head thrust forward and lowered slightly, the hen grouse ran to the side of the road she had started from. Up she hopped into the sapling's sagging branches, where the youngster waited and seemed glad to see her. Then, sitting side by side, peeping face to face, they worked it out.

Now I don't claim to be privy to private grouse talk, but that mother bird must have done some very smooth cooing. After the briefest of tete-a-tetes, a minute perhaps, the matter was resolved. Branch by branch, the hen dropped toward the forest floor. Branch by branch, ever so slightly behind, her trouble maker followed, peeping all the way. Then, without pause, the crossing was made, with mother herding from behind lest there be more second thoughts.

The minute they reached the other side, the two birds disappeared. Maternal clucks ensued as unseen young were reassembled. Then came silence, a slight breeze and camouflage.

A feeling of kinship arose in me as I drove away and the afternoon woods lolled in quiet. 'Nice work, mom,' I said aloud. 'They can drive you up a wall, but they're worth it.'

SOLACE IN A HEAT WAVE

There's been great discussion here lately as to what con-
stitutes a heat wave. Some people think we just had one.
Others don't.

The ones who do constitute any and all humans who
have recently found their stems wilting under a radiant
summer assault that featured unmercifully sticky sheets
and drooping psychological profiles.

The ones that don't are local meteorologists, normal
folks for the most part but prone to playing things by the
book. Sure it's been hot, they say, but not enough for a
heat wave.

'One must read 90 degrees or more on one's shaded thermometer for a number of consecutive days before declaring the presence of a heat wave' is an approximation of
their official decree.

Before a 'cold' front blew into town a few days ago, the daily high temperature in this section of the Northeast had averaged 88 degrees for nearly two weeks. In a flurry of climatic adaptation, the resident human population retaliated by hiding in air-conditioned bedrooms and watching old movies on black-and-white TV. Ice cubes became the major medium of exchange. People were getting up at four A.M. to mow the lawn.

It was broiling hot by ten A.M..

'That's a near heat wave,' the meteorologists said from their hilltop weather station, where winds whistle through wildflowers and the steaming streets of distant Metropolitan City are but a shimmering mirage. 'Close, but no cigar.'

Disappointed to learn there wasn't adequate cause for complaint, we looked to the woods and fields for solace. Perhaps the birds and bees were holding up under the heat in more exemplary fashion than we whining humans with whom they share the outdoors.

It turned out they were. Whether by adapting to summer's solar persistence, or by ignoring it completely, the surrounding flora and fauna had figured out how to survive in style.

Some examples from my July notebook:

The wood thrushes are sleeping these hot days away. We awake at five A.M. and hear their songs wafting from a forest that still holds nocturnal coolness. They will sing for two hours and then stop until almost nightfall. When purple washes the horizon, their soft melodies will resume and we will listen, sitting on the porch feeling almost cool.

Waste place flowers, on the other hand, bake happily in a midday barbecue. 'FULL SUN!' they scream when skies grow momentarily gray. Clumps of hot pink fireweed, giant fuzzy mulleins, sprawling sky-blue chicory - they like their elements hard-edged, even raw. A few rocks, a little dirt, some blazing sun - that's the good life.

A doe and her speckled fawn wait for twilight before meandering through an overgrown field. Grown fat on summer's excessive buffet, they stop to watch and sniff us. We watch back, wishing we could sniff on equal terms. The doe's coat is a soft summer painting, a pastiche of reds and browns as soft as mist on rose petals.

Farther north we watch loons and their fuzzy chicks diving in lakes that are cooler than blacktop cities. We see ospreys circle massive stick nests and hear peeps from young ones housed within. A bullfrog, like some bulbous lily pad sphinx, poses for pictures.

Sparrows spray from the roadside, their weed seed orgies disturbed. Broad-winged hawks spiral upward on noonday thermals. Beavers tow clumps of scrub willow through tepid river shallows.

Heat wave? I guess so, but the natural world, without benefit of a single ice cube, seems slightly less than concerned.

BEWARE THE DAYS OF SUMMER

Beware the days of summer. Between misty dawns and eternal sunsets lies a trap for outdoor compulsives.

An outdoor compulsive is one who is driven to be outside, doing something, for as long as daylight allows. Some of these people are gardeners and golfers; others are hedge clippers and sidewalk trimmers; still others sail, fish and birdwatch.

Compulsives are controlled in December by days that end at five P.M.. Early sunsets force an arbitrary halt to wood cutting, skiing and ice fishing, before exhaustion ensues.

Not so in July, when fifteen-hour days demand that outdoor fanatics temper excess with restraint. Most of them, myself included, fail miserably. There's simply too much freedom. The reins are too loose.

Give us fifteen hours of sunshine, and we react like sweet-toothed kids on a mountain of Mars bars. We see winter as a thirty mile-per-hour zone and summer as a desert highway where speed limits are mere suggestions.

We go totally overboard.

We rise at dawn to grub around in the garden. Robins are hunting worms, their heads cocked like attentive scholars. Catbirds flit through tangles, looking furtive, slightly nervous. Ovenbirds sing from a woodland that is shrouded in mist and pierced by sunbeams.

We coddle perennials and watch zucchinis inflate like rafts. We're glad we got up.

After breakfast we go fishing, not in a secret brook where trout convene beneath undercut banks, but by a river filled with last night's thunderstorm. Along its banks are ostrich ferns, transformed from fiddleheads to giant fronds by the silt of countless floods.

A breeze picks up. Its rhythms surge and fall. Adult mayflies glide downriver, waiting for dry wings and freedom. Dipping, slashing nighthawks are boomerangs carving the sky.

Three blinks of an eye and it's noon. We go sailing, on a Sunfish that begs we find wind and let it push us faster. Gliding, skimming, we hear sounds of speed and water. We see nothing but blue sky and green trees.

Then we stroll on overgrown paths that once were tame but have grown Panamanian. Overhead are peeps and squawks - complaints from nestlings with ceaseless appetites.

Then we picnic, in the back of a pickup, in a field of wild thyme. While children climb white pines and get sap on their hands, adults shave cheese with a jackknife. The thick smell of thyme wafts everywhere.

Then we play softball and watch killdeer scamper through center field. The right fielder fears attack. We reassure him with tales of killdeer kindness.

Then we sit on our deck and wait for the dark. And wait. And wait. It takes forever to get dark these days.

Ever slowly the sky turns from blue to pink to purple. Mars, Saturn, and five hundred fireflies glitter. Crickets rub wings and make music. A final wood thrush stills its fluted song.

Finally, we crawl to bed and crash, exhausted. What if we lived in Alaska, we ponder. That midnight sun would kill us.

AUGUST

FIREWOOD BUDDHA

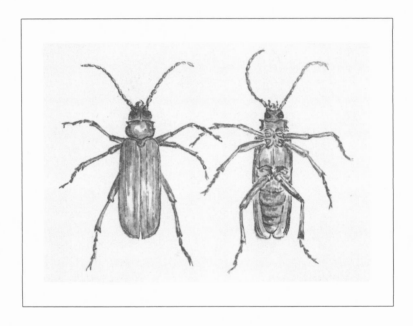

For the past twelve months, sitting in the side yard like a ponderous Buddha, a pile of unsplit firewood has shared my life. It greets me each morning, looming through fog like a tanker in the Strait of Hormuz. It bids me sweet dreams, as moonbeams bounce from its bumpy silhouette and thoughts of Stonehenge boulders and other immovable objects fill my head.

It awaits its destiny with the patience of one who knows that nature is eternal. Someday the ax will appear, a hickory-handled guillotine will creep skyward and a suburban lumberjack will whack the daylights out of butt sections and forked branches.

But the wait is long. Snow drifts gather in the lee of a woodland stump fence. Spring rains roar down streambeds to muddy a floodplain below. Summer days broil while the lumberjack swims and gardens.

Buddha stands ignored.

Finally, ˙during the last week of August, something strange happens. The nights grow cool, the days long-shadowed. Fall is in the air. The woodpile, weathered the light gray of cedar shakes on an ocean shanty, gains dignity.

Chunk by tortuous chunk, it is transformed. The top-most pieces are lugged to the chopping block, bashed into submission and stacked in the garage. The centermost pieces, in the manner of buried stones that are pushed to the surface by frost, move to the top.

Slowly the pile disappears, until, one crisp summer Sunday that smells like October, only bottom chunks remain.

I look at these pieces, the weight of those above them finally removed, and think of human pyramids we once made at the beach. The kids on top were superstars, Peter Pans who always laughed. The ones on the bottom, their feet driven to the ankles in hot sand, were unsung heros. They tried to smile but grimaced.

And so these bottom pieces, mostly large trunk sections a foot or two in diameter, show similar strain. Half-buried in rich topsoil, their smooth gray bark peeling away, they are rotting from the bottom up.

The soil, with its moisture and unseen creatures, will claim title over time. That thin layer between earth and organic log will become a battleground, where life forms feed in the dark.

Grasp a log and wrench it from its mold. Turn it quickly. Watch creatures from a hidden world scurry, burrow and curl from sunlight.

Slugs by the dozen, their mouth parts rasping at rotted cellulose; sow bugs squirming on jointed legs; flat-bodied centipedes dashing after worms with poison claws - all are denizens of damp and shadowed places.

Also scrambling for shelter is a long-horned beetle. Nearly two inches long, with leathery front wings that shine chestnut brown, it scratches for traction on a canvas work glove. It is unhappy, longing to join its larval brethren where they feed on rotting logs.

With each log that is pulled from the soil, scraped of dirt and split for stacking, the long-horn loses habitat. Displaced from a woodpile paradise, it will retreat to adjacent forest where decaying stumps abound.

Perhaps next year will witness another woodpile appear at the side of the house. Perhaps the woodsman will dally again, and the forces of darkness will return in force.

Only time and the seasons will tell.

PIGS IN A TRUFFLE BED

On the hottest days of summer, when school kids wore no shackles and a mirage of aquatic pools shimmered atop every blacktop street, we would walk over to Binghamton's South Washington Street bridge and look down at carp. What we saw, lounging in the tepid Susquehanna River below, were huge, lazy carp, fanning the shallows with tails that swept slowly.

Hanging over a railing that peeled light green paint onto our sunburned forearms, we peered down as the giant fish moved effortlessly upstream in a manner as lethargic as hot summer days.

They were pigs in a truffle bed, those bugle-mouthed monsters. Rooting about in bottom silt with tubular snouts, pushing up mushroom clouds that drifted slowly away in a listless summer flow, they were indelicate and lacking in grace.

We were ten years old and didn't care. The carp were two feet long, beyond our grasp and intriguing beyond words.

We expressed our fascination in ways that, upon adult reflection, were unappreciative. Mostly, we peppered the languishing behemoths with small stones, hoping to bonk one into a burst of aquatic fervor.

Even though we all aspired to baseball immortality, no one seemed able to connect. It must have had something to do with the way water distorts the location of objects that lie beneath it. Not to worry, however. Every once in a while someone would register a near-miss, and Moby Dick, in a listless fit of pique, would sashay upriver, beyond reach of the pip-squeak Ahabs who tormented him.

Therein lay the major drawback in our program of carp bombardment. Before long all the fish within bombing range would move away, leaving us bored, with only ourselves to attack.

Well aware of this inherent flaw, we always hoped to find someone fishing for carp when we arrived at the bridge. Witnessing the primitive spectacle of modern man matching wits with ancient beast was better than a whole afternoon of rock throwing.

Some of the anglers we encountered were European immigrants, who shunned America's disdain for carp as unworthy sport and culinary trash. Others were kids like us, who loathed all piscatorial table fare and would have turned up their noses at salmon in aspic, let alone filet of carp.

The first thing we did upon approaching a bridge fisherman was examine his bait. A man's carp bait, to this day, reflects his relative respect for this golden monster as angling adversary.

Casual fishermen used worms. These people we found boring. Innovative fishermen used a variety of 'stink baits' and other home-baked recipes we found irresistible.

A stink bait is a dough-based concoction that, were it found oozing from a landfill, would be identified as toxic waste. The formula for one might read as follows:

'Peel and grate a potato, add two teaspoons cornmeal, a half teaspoon salt and enough flour and shredded cotton to make a stiff batter. Roll into balls. Cook in boiling water until the balls float. Garnish with a teaspoon of molasses.'

You could smell a good stink bait half way across the bridge. Having been molded around a hook and dropped gingerly into the river, it would immediately release a grease slick of super-tanker proportions.

The carp, rooting in mud downstream, were doomed.

We watched as the slick slithered toward them. We watched as its aromatic tentacles caressed their highly developed olfactory receptors. We held our breath as a five-pound carp sipped the alluring dough ball and moved away to dine in some quiet eddy.

At this point the angler gave a tremendous yank, an elastic groan from stretching line ensued, a massive hippo splash sounded below and the battle was on.

The carp usually rushed down river. The fisherman, forty feet above, would pray he had enough line. If the fish refused to turn, the fisherman would give line more grudgingly and pray again, this time that the line would hold.

This was all breathtaking theatre for the peanut gallery that gaped and hooted while the battle raged. Not until the war was almost over, however, did things get awesome.

Fatigued but still wriggling, its golden scales aglow in sunlight, the carp would be hoisted, ever so carefully, from the river to the bridge above. A giant wrecking ball dangling from a bent fiberglass crane, it would inch its way upward while no one moved lest the line should break.

Once raised aloft, flopping on the bridge's wooden sidewalk slats, the carp became bigger than any youthful imagination: a monster of folklore proportion.

There were lots of afternoons like that, the carp days of summer, when even baseball paled beside life-and-death drama on the bridge. For those memories we thank the mighty carp and revere its name.

The bridge is still there, and so are the fish. Gone, however, are the golden monsters of youth, replaced by smaller fare that only enhance the reputation of those that preceeded them.

I suppose the best course of action would be to forget those carp of yore, but I can't. Every time I walk across that bridge I find myself staring down at the ever-sliding river in hopes of spying a leviathan reborn.

SWALLOWS AND SUMMER RAIN

If you're a barn swallow, then these are fine days, wonderful days of thunderstorms and sweet rain. July has done its job, having run the first lap in a dog day relay. August will take the baton without breaking stride, then speed softly toward September.

If you're a bass, or a butterfly, you're running the relay, too. You are all summer runners, charged with sunlight that spatters forest leaves. You are drawn toward a distant finish line, a line between seasons where frost kills late finishers.

You run toward a winner's circle you may never have seen, that you only feel is there. Those who cross it are judged not by speed but by survival and by offspring produced.

You run but not too fast. Summer tells you to perch in a treetop, to bask on a hot rock, to soar on thermals. It tells you to smell a rose and watch your fellow runners as instinct drives their steps.

Some in the race - like barn swallows - can't step. The only steps permitted these consummate fliers are mincing ones around the rim of their nest when they're young and insecure.

Five such fledglings perch on a nest that sits atop a front porch rafter. They're busting out; they don't fit any more. Parents swoop toward them, landing on a nearby rafter to beckon toward freedom a wingbeat away.

The nestlings balk; they've never flown before. Their tender, white gapes open and close, yammering for food. The parent birds give nothing. They perch five feet away, calling their young toward freedom.

Twelve hours later the nest is empty. Fifty yards away, a telephone line has five new tenants. The fledglings perch there, watching parents chase insects that whir above a nearby pond.

The adults dip on blue-black wings, banking sharply an inch above the water to snap insects human eyes can't see. The youngsters watch. Soon they will dip and snap. Soon they'll succeed.

The western sky builds toward gray and then charcoal. Raindrops, countable at first, splat on dirt roads and car tops. Harder, harder still, they gain force to drench a summer meadow.

Blotted by gardens, collected by ponds, the rain is relished by barn swallows with dusty feathers. A dozen line up on the phone wire, nattering contentedly, bathing in the downpour. Each takes on a load of droplets, then twitches its tail, bobs its head and rubs both wings over its back and sides.

Each one feels the essence of summer.

By thundershower standards, the storm lasts and lasts. For nearly an hour, there is nothing for a swallow to do but perch among the drops feeling cool. There are no insects to catch, no mouths to feed, no lessons to be learned. The pressure is off to race toward a finish line.

There is only rain and a soft hiatus, a time to admire green fields, stare at tassled corn and hear barn swallows talk. There is, as the rain subsides, a moment to hope that summer runners take their time.

BASEBALL UNDER THE LIGHTS

Whenever I think of nighthawks, I remember a ten-year-old boy and baseball under the lights. Night games were a thrill for this child fan. Not only was the grass bathed in luminescence but the rickety wooden ballpark always housed a minor league hero who spit tobacco on dugout steps.

Night baseball was a thrill for parents, too. For fathers, there were cleansing beers after dusty homeplate confrontations. For mothers, with dusk settling dark and pink over the left field fence, there were nighthawks darting among insect swarms that whirled, mesmerized, about stadium lights.

One still remembers lessons from those nights. From the paternal side came subtleties of the double steal, sacrifice, and infield fly; from mother's lips, a sense of respect for winged acrobats that swirled overhead, catching moths in capacious mouths.

Those ballpark nighthawks were my first; I have loved them ever since. Born of the city, at ease with its noise and congestion, they are urban denizens of dignity and class, night riders nesting among crowded streets, then soaring above them in total freedom.

Nighthawks always come to mind at this time of year, because late summer triggers their migration. In looseknit bands that often number several hundred birds, these tireless fliers abandon the northern latitudes and begin meandering south.

Lingering wherever insect morsels appear most abundant, keeping one short step ahead of killing frost, the nighthawk processional wends its way toward Central and South America, where moths abound and Januaries are more understanding.

Watching these flights as they pass overhead, a country observer can't help but notice the angular agility with which nighthawks dip to intercept the smallest of insect prey. Their slender, pointed wings and powerful flight muscles permit endless pursuit of any insect that flies. Bearing down on doomed quarry, they employ huge, dark eyes to track the most convoluted escape attempts without losing focus.

Unseen in a rural setting, however, is the nighthawk's masterful adaptation to the urban nesting grounds it has so successfully colonized. Camouflaged gray and brown, nighthawks blend with the gravel rooftops upon which their equally mottled eggs are deposited without nest or ceremony. Intruders are discouraged by open-mouthed defense postures and broken-wing theatrics.

So well does this sooty flier dovetail with city life that we conclude the two were made for each other. So it may be, but once there were no cities. Nighthawk shadows were a rural sight, knifing over plowed fields and rock-strewn pastureland.

Although the rural nighthawk still exists, its numbers have diminished. The decline coincides with America's rapid urbanization. Perhaps the rural nighthawk fell victim to the lure of city lights - not for the glitter they might promise a restless farmhand, but for the insect bounty of baseball under the lights.

DOES THE HOOK HURT THE WORM?

He asked during a commercial break in *The Dukes of Hazard*, a now-defunct TV show children admired for automotive hijinks. It was an evening in summer, with the windows open and a breeze that smelled like ferns flowing from the woods through our tiny room.

'Can we sleep in your tent?' he asked. 'I'd like to sleep in a tent.'

Lowering the newspaper behind which I had been studiously avoiding eye contact with Bo and Luke Duke, I looked at the boy and felt an important moment happening; a moment I had hoped for, and dreaded, since his birth on a July morning five years ago. He wanted in. He wanted to involve himself with an outdoor world his father held sacrosanct. Now the old man would have to produce. The old man would have to put up or shut up.

'We can...we will,' I said. 'We'll start on the lawn.'

He was pleased and had just begun a stream of questions about goblins and hoot owls when the Dukes came back and swept him away.

I sat behind the paper pondering responsibility. The minute I pound that first tent peg, the minute we crawl into those bags and feel warm flannel, my tenure as outdoor teacher begins. For the next ten or fifteen years, perhaps longer, this boy's questions about the outdoors will be directed at me.

Frustration with camping, fishing, and other skills that look easy but aren't; puzzlement at the apparent cruelty with which nature culls its rejects and reduces surplus; confusion over the line that separates sportsmen from slobs and stewards of nature from its despoilers - the boy will feel all these things. He'll want answers about them, answers I might not have.

The rudiments, the nuts and bolts, will be fun.

This, my son, is a square knot. Use it when you have two pieces of rope and want one. This is the barrel knot. Dad uses it to make tapered leaders for fly fishing. This is a wigwam campfire. You pile your kindling like a teepee. These are Sloppy Joes. These are brook trout in a pan, with wild leeks and butter.

Just drift that worm through the riffle and under that drooping willow. Set the hook now! Good boy! Hold the hatchet this way. Always wet the stone before you sharpen. Paddle, then rest. Don't stand up!

I'll enjoy the questions on nature lore, too. We'll walk in the woods and hear squirrels scolding; I'll talk about territories. We'll go to the swamp in March and watch wood ducks dip through the trees; I'll explain about migration and tell him it's like seeing old friends come back when the woodies return every spring. We'll go out on ocean boats to see sharks and whales for real. We'll hide behind clumps of touch-me-not while hummingbirds sip from tubular bells. We'll split white ash and smell the sap. He'll absorb my reverence for wood.

These will be the fun times, the easy times. The answers to other questions, harder ones, won't come so swiftly.

Why do hunters hunt? Why do deer starve? Do worms feel pain when you stab them with a hook?

Why do some people want to cut forests down and other people want to stop them? Why can't we eat the fish we catch? What are PCBs and mercury?

Outdoor ethics, habitat loss, wildlife conservation versus economic development - all are clouded with debate, confused by undercurrent. None are explained simply. None are grasped easily, even by adults.

Will the boy understand concepts such as no-kill fishing? Will he understand when I say we can keep ten perch for the pan but should release the only rainbow trout we've caught in five hours of trying? Will he understand about imperfect worlds and best-laid plans - how societal flaws manifest themselves in poachers and polluted rivers?

And what of contradictions? Why, he'll ask someday, do we protect the wolf when a century ago we were bent on destroying it? Why do we ban DDT in America but sell it to foreign countries? Why do we mourn for the Atlantic salmon when our own dams and overfishing have caused its demise?

These will be the hard ones. Some of them I don't have the answers for. How will I explain?

I'll be true to myself for starters. If people are cruel or ignorant and wildlife suffers, I'll place the blame where it belongs - on us. If people argue over hunting, or trapping, or clear-cutting, or draining swamps, I'll do my best to give both sides before taking one myself. When talk fails - when I can't convey something in words - I'll try to explain by example.

With luck, the kid will look at me and see something he likes, something he respects. Maybe I won't have to explain everything out loud if what I am, as well as what I say, becomes his cornerstone.

'When can we put up the tent and sleep out?' A round face with smooth cheeks had popped into mine from around the newspaper. The Dukes were gone. The television was silent. Crickets rubbed their legs outside, making soft summer music in the dark.

'We'll put it up tomorrow,' I said. 'While the crickets sing their songs.'

He liked that. So did I.

SEPTEMBER

A TIME TO PREPARE

If you love hot weather, then you're sorry it's September. You're sorry that life without heavy clothes will be over soon. You regret that jumping into ponds and sharing space with bass is becoming chilly business.

It's one of those inevitable seasonal facts: the sun in September is a friend whose visits to the neighborhood have grown shorter and more aloof. No longer do squash vines grow with jungle quickness. No longer does the fireball burn at lunchtime and refuse to die at night.

It's a colder fire that burns in the sunset these days, as

if someone in the southern hemisphere has offered Mr. Sol free use of a beach house on the Peruvian coast, and the old boy's dying to be gone.

The nights are short, the shadows long. Sun rays strike diffused blows that warm but refuse to permeate. What were endless days have become short bursts of warmth into which we cram last gasps of easy living.

As the chill increases, we ransack closet corners where sweaters have languished in seasonal exile. We drape blankets over the back of the couch, comforters on the foot of the bed.

We prepare.

The dog has taken to curling on the carpet. She's abandoned linoleum. It feels cold - not cool - in the night. The cat naps in early morning sun, absorbing it like a sphinx with dead batteries. Her fur a shade thicker than yesterday, her muscles limbering, she acknowledges the solar charge with an occasional stretch.

And then there's us. We must slay the woodpile, sauce the tomatoes, can the pickles, knit the sweaters, caulk the windows. The essence of September is in getting ready.

Wild creatures are getting ready, too, only on a much tighter schedule. Seasonal change rules their lives. Transitions are short, results immutable. Slackers of glade and glen are assured only of death. None live to transfer genetic poison.

The gigantic toad that lives by the woodpile looks like a slacker but isn't. An amphibious touring sedan of bumps and beady eyes, this creature has been slowed by cold mornings to a speed approaching no speed at all.

Lumbering through the damp grass, feeling a chill that can only worsen with October, the bug-spearing patriarch can't even hop over a work boot. He bumps and goes around.

Waste no more days, my toad friend. Soon nights will come when burrowing underground will be your only defense against a season toads never see.

Wait for high noon, when your engine finally warms. Stalk your cricket prey as the heron stalks the minnow: with the patience of statues. Flick your tongue and swallow. Grow fat.

Then find a spot where soft soil makes burrowing easy; where a toad of ample girth can dig down and disappear, down into the soil, away from ice and cold. Tend to these matters now, for the time of hard ground will come soon. Soon, but not today. Today is warm. There's still time. Time to prepare.

SO CLOSE TO REAL PERFECTION

What is perfection, and how long must it last to be real?

Is it a river valley on the last day of summer, when the skies are bluer, the breezes fresher and the flowers brighter than they've ever been?

Can it come and go in a single earthly spin, in a burst of sunlight that gleams on quiet pools and turns tree leaves into gold coins?

It is, and it can. You need only place yourself there, taking deep breaths and turning your face toward the sun, to believe.

And where is this place, this Shangri-la where perfection smiles and bird songs, not car horns, are the status quo?

It's a lot of places, really. It's anywhere that doesn't have a building more than two stories high. It's anywhere you can sit on a road, hear a car go by, and hear silence again. It's anywhere far from four-lane highways, where drivers speed by oblivious, caring only about getting there, not about things on the way.

To experience perfection, you must go to this place, unpack your bag and stay at least one day. This will preclude your rushing about, demanding that cellophane-wrapped, made-for-TV dose of sylvan aesthetics many think is real.

And don't leave your engine running. Turn it off. Wander about with no destination. Take your watch and your deadline brain and your five-minute updates, and hide them.

Then open your eyes and think about what you see.

You'll see hills that pile themselves along the river like well-worn vertebrae. They're turning colors while you watch, but slowly. You wish, just once, your mind was a time-lapse camera.

Wander off the road and into a tangled field. Revel in the yellow of goldenrod, the purple of New England aster. No bouquet anywhere, no matter what time of year, can soak in sunlight and bounce it back with such brilliance. These purples and yellows will perform in full costume until summer's final curtain. Tomorrow, perhaps, the frost will creep; tomorrow the dark and brutal finale. Today is bright color in sunlight.

Before a late afternoon chill takes hold, abandon the sun and walk in the woods. Look up. Black cherries have ripened to a purple that borders on black. Cedar waxwings find them and feast.

Wild grape clumps are ready, too, sagging from vines that probe with tentacle fingers. Taste a grape; make a face. Too sour? Maybe for you, but not for grouse that will gather here come October.

By now it's well past noon. Stand on a bridge, watch the water slide by and think of a season when no creature alive lacks for food. The fruit of the land is everywhere.

Then pour some milk, put a sandwich on a paper plate and sit where the sun shines. Monarch butterflies will drift lazily across a landscape that seems relaxed and satisfied. The pressure is off now; that's the message of late September. Summer has nothing left to prove.

If possible, spend the rest of the afternoon splashing along the riverbank. Wonder aloud if small-mouthed bass and rainbow trout have felt the chill of changing seasons and slipped toward deeper water. Listen as chipmunks chip, chip, chip to solidify the sanctity of winter dens. Watch as a doe leads her twins across the river. Baby spots are gone. Coats grow thick and brown.

When you feel warm in the sunlight but cold in the shade, head back to a tiny crossroads hamlet where they've been painting a church. Autumn's coming on, the painters say. Last chance to paint a church.

There's a tavern at the crossroads that wants you to stop and sit awhile. Inside is an ancient pot-bellied stove with a good, slow burn on - just right for warming hands when nights get cold.

Relax. Don't be in a hurry to leave this pool-tabled place. These are good country people with a proper sense of time and transition. Talk about the weather a lot and the river a little. Then say goodnight.

As you walk down the road, be glad there aren't street lights. Let the night sky surround you with millions of stars, a sprawling celestial mass. Don't separate them by constellations. Take them all in as one.

Your destination, somewhere in the darkness, is a tiny fishing shack with no heat or indoor plumbing. Go inside, cook a trout, and talk about the river some more.

Fumble with a sleeping bag and get in. Feel it warm on the inside, cool on the outside. Lie in the dark and ponder perfection in late September.

Then close your eyes and dream, knowing stars still shine on the river.

A DOZEN WINGED JACKKNIVES

This is the story of a lawyer who knew a great deal about libel suits and not quite so much about birds.

One afternoon a distinguished counselor-at-law swiveled away from a deskful of books with no pictures, rubbed his brief-weary eyes and gazed out a tenth story window.

To sue or not to sue; to settle or not to settle - the barrister ruminated on the day's docket of legal affairs. Perhaps a show-cause order would be best, or even a subpoena. His legal wheels spun in counterpoint to the drone of distant dictaphones and typewriters chattering legalese.

It was a flash of motion outside the window - a gray blur on a sooty skyline - that wrenched him from the reveries for which he was so handsomely remunerated. Speeding through the air, some five stories below, were a dozen winged creatures with movements too intriguing to ignore.

Like so many flying cigars, they fluttered over blacktop roofs below, first veering into sharply banked turns, then stalling in flight as Piper Cubs might at a small-town air show. While the attorney watched with growing interest, several of the birds nose-dived toward a huge brick chimney, there to be sucked within by an unknown magnetism.

Now some might say that lawyers, with their artificial language and all, can't relate to the natural world. Too many 'herewiths,' the critics claim, and not enough 'how comes.'

Watching a dozen winged jackknives slice through the sky, this particular lawyer proved them wrong.

'What are those things?' he wondered. 'Are they birds? Are they bats? Why do they seem so fascinated with that big chimney?'

His sword of curiosity undulled by countless battles with verbal puffery, the counselor didn't have answers but wanted them.

A telephone call to an acquaintance of more naturalistic bent ensued.

'They're chimney swifts,' the acquaintance replied, having heard the lawyer's account, 'and you're right, they look a lot like bats. They're flying around the chimney because their nests are inside it. The nests are glued to the chimney walls with a sticky saliva the swifts produce especially for the purpose.'

If he had heard more than he wanted to about chimney swifts, the attorney didn't say. In fact, the stimulus of a nature-related discussion seemed to inspire him toward greater inquisitive heights.

'Maybe these birds are what caused my spiders to disappear,' he said. 'For years, there always were spiders on the window sill, but lately there aren't any. Maybe the birds ate the bugs that the spiders needed for food, and the spiders moved on.'

The naturalist fell silent, momentarily stunned. This man was a thinker. It's not every lawyer who is up on his intra-food chain population dynamics.

'That's an interesting theory,' the bird man replied, regaining composure. 'Chimney swifts do eat a great many insects - and the odd spider as well. Under normal circumstances, however, there should be enough bugs to feed both spiders and chimney swifts.'

I'm comforted to find that out,' the attorney said.

The naturalist believed him.

WHILE INFANTS DREAM

My daughter, a tiny thing not yet two, has deep brown eyes that verge on black. One gazes toward them and melts. They are dark, friendly pools, filled with innocence. They tell you the person surrounding them needs love and expects you to give it.

All summer long, circling over this little girl's room, were two broad-winged hawks. As she slept the afternoon away, exhausted from tearing up the house, they circled on wings that made sport of metal flight.

Broad-winged hawks, as it happens, also have brown eyes, but they are hazel brown, with a touch of red. They are bird-of-prey eyes - large, acute, self-reliant. Speaking not of kindness but of strength and survival, they will not be intimidated. They will stare you down.

As the little girl slept, sunshine beamed down on these broad-wings. It emboldened their silhouettes, highlighting black and white bands on their tails. Retiring, crow-sized birds of the hardwood forest, they had sought out open sky as a backdrop for courtship flights. These flights began on a day in mid-May, with both birds transcribing lazy circles that had equal diameters but carved blue space on different planes.

The first circles were tight and disciplined. Then came a widening, as the birds fell away and became distant specks on opposite sides of the sky. For several minutes they orbited on their own, independent.

Suddenly the broad-wings swooped toward one another. No longer did their wings float outstretched on invisible updrafts. Now they were streamlined, folded close to the body. The birds slit through cumulous pillows on a journey toward commitment.

The pair flashed toward impact, two runaway trains on the same line of track. Imagine how their eyes must have glowed as they streaked to within ten feet of each other, swooped upward at the last second and hung suspended as if to marvel at their own fluidity. Imagine the nuptual bond such aerial mastery must have forged between them.

After watching that first flight, I shared the broad-wing ritual every day for two weeks. The birds would let me know they were there by calling to one another.

Pweee-eeee. A high-pitched whistle would come around noon. I would look up and watch.

The diving and swooping finally stopped in early June, when the birds retired to assume household chores at a nest on a nearby ridge. They still would soar overhead, but the flights were infrequent and lacked hormonal fire.

A month ago, the broad-wings and their youngsters moved south. They awaited a north wind and let it sweep them toward Central America. I look forward to their return already. There would be a great emptiness if they didn't turn up in the sky next May.

Making the wait a bit easier is my confidence that the broad-wings will return. Laws now protect them. People understand how birds of prey help control rodent populations; how they help keep an ecosystem in balance. How they belong.

Not all people understand, but so many more than years ago.

Call it selfish, but I want broad-wings over my house long after I'm gone. I want their lazy circles long after the forest around me has aged, crumbled and sprouted again. For starters, I'll be thrilled just to see them return next May, to watch the girl with the brown eyes grow.

OCTOBER

AUTUMN IN ITS GLORY

Set your sights on an island in a huge inland lake. Paddle toward it at dawn and feel stirrings that are autumnal, filled with change.

The island is black, a wisp of rock and sedge amidst miles of open water. Fog swirls around it, herded over choppy waves, pushed westward by an easterly wind. A crescent moon beams from above with astonishing clarity, cradled by earth's near-circular shadow.

The fog yields quiet gabblings, peeps of welcome for another day.

Your boat strikes rock. A whirring ensues, a bursting of duck bodies from repose toward vertical flight. Mallards most likely, maybe a black duck or two. There's no way of knowing. Their quacks are identical, their wingbeats the same on a background of sunrise pink.

The mallards among them are summer residents, grown fat on smartweed and corn. The black ducks have come from farther north, nurtured on remote beaver ponds, driven south by a cold front threatening sleet instead of summer rain.

The closest of puddle duck relatives, these dabblers will stay several more weeks, until new cold fronts arrive and shoreline sloughs freeze hard. Only then will they push deeper down, toward the Chesapeake and Long Island Sound.

Another bird wave arises, flattens out, then slices fog on angled wings. Streamlined at one end by trailing feet, at the other by long pointed bills, they are greater yellow-legs, ideals of form and movement. Born of the tundra, blessed with instinctive wanderlust, they master the wind, knifing through it.

Off they go, streaking toward mudflats on a distant shore. Soon stilts will wade through shallows, while bills probe muck for snails. Soon boilers will be fueled and fat layers augmented. Tomorrow may dawn on birds winging south toward Sanibel. Today finds them here, flying low through the fog, calling *wheu-wheu-wheu* in flutelike tones.

Sit still on the island, alone, watching dawn. The sun has crept higher, adding brilliance to red and sugar maples already aflame on a distant shore. Crunch a local apple, sweet and perfect. Lie back. Let sunlight warm your face.

Like this apple, red and shining, the season has ripened. Canada geese will wing through the afternoon, so high up they might touch cirrus clouds. Their honks will sound faintly, a garbled conglomerate. Their destination beckons from somewhere beyond, somewhere closer to night-fall.

Bathed in warmth, curled in a boat with sedge blades rustling gently, you'll sleep through the afternoon, awakening to watch a lone snow bunting comb rocks for errant seeds. The wind will have freshened. Waves will slap a naked shore.

Only at twilight will the yellowlegs return. They're sure to this night, because fall has been mild thus far. They and the ducks will come back, landing silently as darkness falls, tucking heads beneath wings and sleeping to lullabies of waves and autumn in its glory.

THE SOUND OF GNAWING TEETH

Perhaps a wisp of scent filled the beaver's nose with danger. Perhaps we had brushed a scrub willow, and rodent ears had heard. Whatever it was, it blew our cover.

Swimming in ever-tightening circles, the beaver knew it had company. An outside presence had disturbed the pond's natural rhythm; a presence unnerving to those that called this labyrinth home.

'Crack!'

A report of gunshot clarity broke the silence, echoed off a side hill and dissolved. We stood stock still and listened.

'Crack!'

The beaver struck again, its tail slap resounding like an iron dinner plate. We still didn't move, alone with the guilt of our trespass.

The standoff continued. Swimming to within five feet of the pond edge, the beaver would slap, dive, resurface, then slap again. Tacit intruders stayed quiet, pretending they weren't there and thinking beaver thoughts.

Why didn't the beaver just dive and disappear for good? Why swim about, in the face of danger, when there was mud to mold in more remote sections of this watery maze?

The answer lay just behind us, in a trembling aspen grove. Throughout the stand, freshly cut saplings littered the ground like fallen matchsticks. Their exposed heart-wood sections gleamed ghostly white. Fresh outer bark smelled sweet and green.

Last night, as part of the flurry of tree felling that precedes each winter season, curved incisors had cut through these aspens as chisels might through the softest pine. Tonight, the owner of said teeth was back, intent on finishing the job of dragging the saplings into the pond for storing underwater as winter food.

Here we were in the way.

A seeping chill ended that. We began shivering, our heavy pants proving no match for impending darkness. The beaver swam back and forth, its guard hairs trapping air, repelling water, defying the cold.

He had all night. We had five minutes. It was no contest.

We halted our retreat only once, to look down on the pond from a nearby knoll. Purple streaked the horizon. A wood duck dipped in from nowhere, weaving easily through tree silhouettes. Hooded mergansers squawked hoarse, twilight messages, then settled into sleep and a thickening fog.

Somewhere near the pond edge, gnawing methodically, beaver teeth went to work.

WOOD WARMS YOU TWICE

Whoever said, 'Splitting wood warms you twice,' certainly knew how to make hard work sound like fun. The tongue-in-cheek woodsman could have said, 'Splitting wood gives you a sore back and aching forearms,' but that wouldn't have been nearly as clever, and no one would have remembered it. So he stuck with the euphemistic approach, and, as a result, millions of latter-day Paul Bunyans are woefully unprepared for that first mighty swat at a stone-hard chunk of knots and twisted grain they envision as fuel.

As the splitting maul bounces back, its handle vibrating like a devining rod gone mad, a suburbanite might wish he hadn't gone quite so far back to nature. Thoughts of oil trucks creep from banishment. Bunyanesque resolve dwindles.

For that poor soul, the following words are designed to highlight the positive side of the wood chopper's madness, while reinforcing his decision to follow a splintery road toward warmth in winter.

There is darkness but no dawn as our woodsman stares at what lies before him. Huge cross-sections of ash, beech, and hickory lie in a jumbled pile, sullenly awaiting their rendezvous with maul and battered wedge. They promise to warm the winter hearth, but not without a fight.

Once the battle begins, there are as many close-grained victories as gnarled defeats. Blocks of beechwood, boasting steely veneers, are quickly transformed into clean-cut wedges of cherry-colored pie. Split remains of shagbark, when pressed to the nose, smell damp and fresh, like saddle soap, bridles, horsebarns and hay. A white ash log splits with a snap as the wedge cleaves its light brown heartwood. Those are the good times.

On other occasions, when the woodpile bristles with forked branches and buried knotholes, man's reverence for wood may not provide adequate inspiration. At that point, it's best to step back, revive drooping spirits, and absorb an outdoor world that rustles with change.

Overhead, obscured by mist, blue sky struggles to free itself. Wine-red leaves drift down, their stems detached by last night's killing frost. Along the wood edge, a tattered mourning cloak butterfly flutters in search of a hibernation place. Blue jays, quiet for a change, gorge on white oak acorns. Cardinals dash among half-bare branches, their sharp calls muffled in fog.

Inside the house, black cherry burns, hissing in smoky surrender, resigned to warming a woodsman for the second time.

GOLDEN EAGLE WINGS

It started with a football game, the non-violent kind where a father chases a son, a son chases a father, and one of the two gets tired.

It ended with golden eagle wings, long and flat, carving blue space.

In the middle were about three minutes of wonder.

That's all it took - three minutes - for a speck to appear on the northern horizon, soar overhead on glider wings and disappear beyond an oak-topped ridge to the south.

A lot happened during those three minutes. They faded quickly but stick in the mind as frozen moments; brief, timeless, moments between an average person and a special predatory bird.

Size was the spark that ignited this football-addled brain.

'That creature up there is bigger than a red-tailed hawk,' the brain thought. 'Much bigger.'

The eagle's wings were ironing boards, stretched flat to maximize lift. At their tips were primary feathers, flared to hitch the free ride a northerly breeze provided. Approaching by degrees, the eagle loomed larger, not moving a muscle, going somewhere south with steadiness.

The kid, a sneaky sort, tried an end run and scored. I called time out and looked straight up. An incredible soaring machine was 200 feet above me, with sunlight beating on it. I saw a broad band of white at the base of the tail. Single "windows" of white splashed each underwing. The rest was imposing silhouette, dark brown and streamlined on brilliant blue sky.

'Delay of game - golden eagle,' I shouted, rushing inside for binoculars. The boy stood there, perplexed, wanting to kick extra points.

'Eagle over the house!' I was inside now, hollering up the stairs. My mate, ensnared in a potty-training session with a two-year-old, could not break away. 'Then stick your head out the window,' I said. 'It's dead overhead.'

It wasn't when I got back out. It had glided farther south but was still within view. The binoculars confirmed wing and tail field marks that identified this eagle as immature; a year old, perhaps, maybe two.

A rare find east of the Mississippi, golden eagles are mysterious birds, thought to nest here, thought to nest there, never getting pinned down. Preferring open mountains, foothills, and plains, a few goldens breed in the Appalachians, but where is another story.

Where it came from, where it was going - I didn't think about all that while the eagle soared overhead. I didn't think much at all, really. I just looked up, taking mental pictures for scrapbooks down the road.

Smaller, smaller, smaller, gone. The golden eagle - maybe the only one I'll ever see without leaving the front yard - had topped a red oak ridge and departed my life. My fellow bird watcher, just six years old and not really into eagles, kicked the extra point and won his ninth game in a row, 7-6.

Home is a wonderful place, I thought, especially when eagles come calling and let you watch them fly.

NOVEMBER

AS HILLSIDES LOSE THEIR FIRE

By this time of year, anyone who's going to Florida has already gone. Those of us with ties that bind wave good-bye and ponder hillsides that have lost their fire.

We look back at October's first weeks and remember the bright colors, the hot sun. We look ahead to November and imagine its turkey dinners, its comforting hearth. We commune with trees that speak a language of skeletons. They no longer block the wind.

And then, if we're smart, we look down at our feet and contemplate the present, a world of damp and fallen leaves, of change and fermentation.

This place, where October meets November, offers tastes of past and future. There are backward glances at soft nights and flowers; first chances to feel wool and goose down again. The October in us remembers summer. The November knows winter coming on.

Our world changes radically as we tread this transitional ground. One day, we're private, still enwrapped in a leafy shroud. The next, we are open, exposed. We can see distant lights, and they can see us.

Our new, more public existence, allows us to look out the window for miles, through bare branches that revive the world's forgotten contours. Below us, our hill tumbles toward a distant floodplain. A mile or so above, its rounded crest mingles with rain clouds. We sit somewhere in the middle, perched on the side of a large topographical bowl.

We scrutinize the hill as if we had never seen it before. We follow its spinal ridgetops, where oak leaves shake and fall. Our eyes become hands, smoothing its sundry bumps and saddles, feeling where the glacier didn't scrape so hard.

We note its V-shaped grooves, where other hills have joined it in a blend of rounded forms. The grooves tell us streams are there, floating leaves toward flatland rivers.

Then we wander through a leafless landscape, remembering, after six months of dense foliage, how much fun it is to watch gray squirrels scamper on the roof of the forest. They defy an arboreal tight wire. Their claws never miss.

Everything on the hill is easier to see. Nut trees no longer hide their bounty; acorns, butternuts and hickory nuts all hang in silhouette.

Blue jay beaks grasp the acorns like pliers. Butternuts, with sticky brown husks, are gathered by farmers and placed in pails on the porch. Hickory nuts fall on driveways and rumble when cars crush their shells.

Around twilight, on our hill, the migrant birds arrive. Tired from flying toward a warmer winter, they seek food first and then shelter - shelter from owls' eyes that glow like yellow moons.

Robins appear overhead in loose flocks. They land high in a white oak, chirping comforting chirps, preening their pumpkin breasts. Juncos prefer lower playgrounds, dashing about in thornapples, stopping to scratch at a feeder that's just opened for business.

White-throated sparrows flit through the scrub, plundering a gray dogwood's off-white berries. The white-throats sing their beautiful song, but it falls apart in mid-sentence.

Just before dark, before an ever-quickening sunset flames and disappears, a woodcock flutters by. Its long, probing bill points downward. Huge brown eyes search the hillside for a friendly aspen grove where worms will fuel southern flight.

The woodcock feels November as we never can. It will stop on the hill only briefly; tonight, perhaps, but gone tomorrow.

Tonight, as the woodcock rests, we'll watch the autumn stars. The sky will be very big, the chill of a colder season very real.

TRACKING DEER

They were arrowheads without shafts, deer tracks piercing freshly fallen snow. They wandered through a long-abandoned apple orchard, crossed a stream that tumbled crooked and semi-frozen, then slipped through a stand of white pines that glowered in dark, gray shadow. I followed, staring at the ground, reading puzzles.

How big was this deer? Not very. A doe of eighty pounds might have made these tracks; a yearling buck of ninety. How frightened was it? Not frightened at all. The impressions were a foot apart as their maker ambled through a tangle of goldenrod.

How far ahead was the deer? How many arrowheads kept us apart? I saw nothing, heard nothing, yet somehow felt a closeness.

One cloven hoof at a time, one step following another, the tracks entered a forest of tree trunk soldiers. The pines stood densely packed, all on tiptoes to capture light from above. Dead lower branches had lost the battle for sunbeams. Their sole purpose now was to poke an eye or snap so loud as to scare every deer for miles.

The deer I followed had walked softly, its nimble forelegs lifting and falling without snapping twigs. A coal black muzzle had glistened, with nostrils flared for danger on the wind. Ears had twitched; a head had snapped when pine cones fell. The air filled with expectation.

Ahead lay evidence of rest and calm: a bare patch beneath the pines where body heat had melted snow to expose a needle carpet. Sleep had come here, a respite from vigilance. These conifers meant shelter not only from wind and snow but from human predators.

The deer bed felt cold. No deer had heard me seconds before. No deer had leapt crashing through stumps and blowdowns. There was time between us. The tracks lead away, winding through dead branch flotsam. I followed on ponderous feet.

A band of chickadees pecked on tree trunks, buzzing cheerfully. Golden-crowned kinglets fluttered in midair, hovering over branches in search of larval sleepers. A red squirrel scolded a quiet world, then ran away on pine bough stepping stones.

I lost the tracks. I found them again, huge spaces in between with needles churned on contact. The tracks crossed a crumbled wall of stones, then bounded through hardwood glades that once were fields. I saw a deer in my mind, bounding without effort, leaping with hooves outstretched. I saw fluidity given definition, oxygen molecules brushed aside without friction.

The tracks broke through a pine woods perimeter, angled down a steep ravine, approached a meandering brook and disappeared. My deer trail had vanished. A bond had broken. I was alone.

Had the deer wandered downstream, walking in water, leaving no tracks? Had it bolted upstream, panicked by human sounds behind it? I checked both banks, upstream and down, for fifty yards and found nothing.

An hour later I sat in a forest tent feeling warm against the gray and gloom. The lantern glow was golden, the stove heat comforting. Spanish rice steamed on a Coleman burner as we talked of pocket knives and trout streams, fireplace wood and toboggans through deep snow.

Outside - quite close, probably - was a creature I had followed but might never know. In the corner were a cot and sleeping bag, where soon I would dream of deer that were magic.

THE FIRST TIME IT SNOWED

As far as cultural curiosities are concerned, the American Happy Hour has pretty much passed me by.

It's not that I'm not a Happy Hour kind of guy. I'm happy, for example, when it starts to get dark on Friday afternoon, and secretaries put egg-warmers over their typewriters. I also feel the faintest of gender-related kinship with those guys on TV who end the work week by rushing toward pubs to ogle winking coquettes.

Kinship aside, however, I just don't "do" Happy Hour that often. Maybe it's the cigarette smoke, or my farm-oriented demeanor that keeps me away from two-for-one drinks, you-shuck-'em shrimp, and Maurice at the piano bar. I really don't know.

Whatever the cultural barriers, they all came tumbling

down on a night in early November when, with the fascination of an anthropologist in a Borneo subculture, I entered a local oasis to observe loose-as-a-goose natives celebrating the temporary cessation of work week bondage.

It was the first night all year that it snowed.

Snow wasn't falling at first. It had been cold on the way over from work - with a chilling wind that flapped the Jeep's canvas windows like tents on an Arctic fairground - but it wasn't snowing.

Inside the oasis, by contrast, native bodies were packed together. A communal rise in temperature ensued. We ordered dry sarsaparillas, straight up, with an olive.

The place had one of those busy, eclectic decors, created perhaps by an oil sheik with a yen for American bric-a-brac who had just been to a garage sale.

The libation was good, however, and as I gazed from one mingling native to the next, my eye seized on a window and glimpses of night outside.

Crystal flakes descended, their whiteness heightened by spotlights from a car lot nearby. Landing on Caprice Classics and Fairmont four-doors, the flakes linked hexagonal sides to form a fluffy mass reminiscent of electric train mountains.

This was real snow, however. I had to walk outside.

'Don't get so excited,' my companion said, snuggling his long-stemmed glass. 'Just because you're tuned to the seasons doesn't mean everyone else has to be.'

He was right. The natives weren't at all excited. They were too busy popping balloons to get notes inside that announced prizes for lucky winners. 'A free roll of toilet paper!' our note exclaimed.

Outside, glorified by used car lights, the first snow of the year was falling. It would stop in two hours, amounting to little save a gentle reminder that God hadn't forgotten how dual hemispheres work.

Only a thin, patchy blanket would remain by morning. Not enough to shovel, already dripping from the roof in big drops that smacked against gutters, it would be gone by noon and disappoint little boys seeking snowmen.

There would be just enough to clump on pine boughs and then slide off; just enough to sit on the wood pile without soaking in; just enough to show squirrel footprints.

Then it would melt away, willing to wait just a little longer until calendar pages told colder stories.

Inside the oasis, natives were cozy and warm. They communicated lustily with noisemakers as we bid them farewell and walked through snowflakes to the car.

Is it really so strange, I thought on the way, to be tuned to the seasons?

No, I thought back. Go home and put wood on the fire. Feel good about winter coming on.

A TIMELESS INGREDIENT OF CHANGE

It's been a mild and patient autumn, but the hills aren't orange any more, and there are certain things in nature no one can change. One of them we call winter.

We've had our Indian summer. Through October and November, we've been granted an extension on storm window deadlines that has been generous beyond reason. Let's not ruin everything by praying it will last forever.

There's no such thing as eternal fall in these latitudes. Only a fool would count on autumn stopping winter's inexorable emergence from Arctic staging grounds. A more beneficial outlook might be to seek in the late autumn landscape a lesson in change and adaptation. As the winter solstice approaches, there's not one wild creature alive wasting time hoping it will take a wrong turn. Each is preparing for the inevitable. By watching them, we can prepare as well.

There's a ground rule, however. Viewing seasonal change through a storm window can be less than satisfying. Late autumn demands closer scrutiny.

Take a walk, a little walk. Peer at this calendar page of frost and wood smoke with appreciative eyes and an open mind. As well as offering the universal lessons inherent in all seasons, it may reveal special ones of its own.

Watch a whitetail buck walk hedgerows at dusk with his doe and yearling band. Antlers curl to sharpened points. Guard hairs lie sleek and flat, slate gray like November skies. The does leap in unison at a snapped twig, bounding across a clearing with the spring of pogo sticks. The buck waits, with a caution that may save him on a day when hunters walk these hills.

Walk back toward home, to study a firewood pile. Check each log for dryness. Split a piece of red oak, smell its tannic freshness and know it isn't ready. Throw it toward the back, toward February or March.

Pet a cat that sleeps in the barn. She curls in a ball, wrapped in fur and dreams. Look for a lone breast feather that bobs among lakeshore cattails. It says a mallard was here at dawn, feeding while you slept. Find a muskrat's river catacomb, the tunnel labyrinth that snakes beneath undercut sycamores, sheltering muskrat eyes from those of great horned owls. Tell wind direction by watching chimney smoke.

Do these things, and you might not begrudge winter its turn. Perhaps you'll see it from a broader perspective, more as a timeless ingredient of change than a reminder of how far humans have removed themselves from the cycle of seasons.

DECEMBER

THE TALE OF DY-DEE MAN

There is, I've discovered, a cosmic connection between wet diapers and hungry birds. To understand how such disparate spheres spin toward synchronicity, one must enter the world of newborns, where there exists, for harried parents, a white knight in a tidy van: the Dy-Dee man.

If you pay the Dy-Dee man what he wants, he will arrive at your door once a week at 7 A.M. with a fresh load of diapers. All he asks, upon arrival, is that the ones he brought last week are waiting for him outside the garage door.

Under normal conditions, Dy-Dee man rides tall in the saddle. Galloping through one sleepy town after another, grabbing up wet diapers and leaving dry ones behind, he is the Pony Express personified.

There is only one thing that slows Dy-Dee man down; one thing in which he lives in constant fear: a mountainous driveway covered with glacier-like ice floes and enough frozen, snowball sized boulders to discourage an Everest attack force.

Loving Dy-Dee man as we do, and needing him so desperately, we try our best to avoid presenting him with this kind of roadway. Sometimes, it can't be avoided.

When it rains, freezes, snows, melts, snows, rains and freezes again, our poor friend must gird his loins and fight the uphill fight.

One December morning, I vowed to spare the thankless warrior a terrifying ascent by waking before sunrise and dragging his diaper load to the bottom of the hill. Although good will was an important consideration in plotting this move, I admit to ulterior motives. Birds would be stirring in the pre-dawn stillness. They would be opening their eyes, puffing their feathers and drifting like shadows toward feeders with sunflower seeds. If I walked quietly, they would let me watch.

A pair of cardinals came first. Dipping through thornapple with erratic twists, nervously popping their crests to attention and back, they landed in a bare red maple to survey the scene.

The brilliance of male cardinals is hardly diminished by lack of direct sunlight. Bright red birds on steel-gray branches in pre-dawn stillness - could any painting be as vivid?

The cardinals dropped to the ground and hopped beneath our hanging feeder, where spilled sunflower seeds dotted hardened snow like sprinkles on vanilla cones. They poked and scratched about, snapping seeds with their fat bills, looking nervous but nutritionally sound.

A downy woodpecker knocked stoically on frozen suet; juncos and tree sparrows sneaked from nearby bushes to fuel tiny boilers with smashed corn kernels; titmice arrived already fueled, with half-pint scoldings and fire in their shiny black eyes.

Charcoal clouds pinkened with first light. The world would wake up serene.

There developed, rather rapidly, a splotch on this pastiche of pastoral perfection. It was automotive in nature, arriving with a great gnashing of gears at the bottom of the driveway. It was Dy-Dee man, engine whining, tailpipes roaring, come to save us.

Birds erupted from all sides and fled for the woods. Dogs barked from bedroom confinement. Albert and the Chipmunks sang loudly about Christmas from a radio in the tidy van.

Dy-Dee man, his breath puffing in cheery white clouds, was grateful we spared him the driveway. Parked at the bottom, he switched good diapers for bad, hopped back in the van, and departed on his next mission with a wave that made me think of the Lone Ranger and Paul Revere.

Watching him gallop into the dawn, I felt as grateful as he did - for the diapers, of course, and for the birds.

WINTER WALK

The hardest thing about enjoying the outdoors in winter is getting outdoors in the first place.

First light on a wintry Saturday finds you buried under homemade quilts. Just sticking out is your nose, a thermometer of sorts that estimates house temperature by twitching back and forth. On this morning, frost is forming on the old snoot. The stove must have died overnight.

You stumble downstairs seeking firewood. Indoor supplies are exhausted; you must go to the woodshed for more. Better check a real thermometer before you dash out. Six degrees!

The sprint from house to shed and back is completed in record time. You can almost see the cold as it envelopes your ankles; a silent cold that reminds you you're ill-equipped to survive.

Back in the house, your robe front sprinkled with wood chips, you restart the dwindled fire. Fifty-five... fifty-eight... sixty-two. Warmth returns to the house by degrees.

Staggering back upstairs, you notice dawn breaking, then decide it's too cold to stay up. Icy feet are plunged under covers. A vow is made: not to come out for three days.

By mid-morning that vow has been broken. The house is warm and smells like bacon. Little boys play with Teddy bears and toy farm cows. Sunlight streams through the window, feeding Norfolk Island Pines. Perhaps you could force yourself out for just a short meander.

Snow crunches underfoot as you walk the stump fence trail. Clouds of breath determine wind direction: straight from the west in bursts.

Animal tracks are everywhere. Deer have tramped through the garden, their V-shaped tracks molded hard in the snow. A white-footed mouse must be living in the old bluebird house. Its tiny tracks lead right to the nest box pole and disappear. Here's a spot where a ruffed grouse landed. You can see where its wingtips hit the snow.

Crunching along, you can't help but notice bird nests, each covered with a snow-white top hat. Strongest of all is the goldfinch's woven abode, a thistledown affair no storm can rip asunder.

The crows are out today. Two land in a sprawling white oak to survey their frozen domain. *Caw! Caw! Caw!* You've tried to find their roost for years. Maybe in March you'll succeed.

Your feet begin to fail; they're always the first to get cold. It's all right, though. You knew this would be just a short walk, a time for taking breaths, watching birds, and feeling friendly about winter again.

Cherub cheeks press on a window as you stride within view of the house. The rest of the day will be spent fixing toys and telling stories. Tomorrow will bring chances for another walk. It might even be warmer by then.

HE BOTHERED WHITE-FOOTED MICE

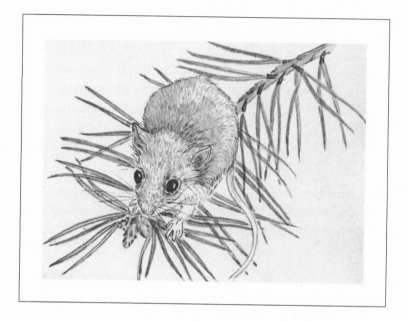

They'll say of me some day: 'He made a career of bothering white-footed mice.' It happened again recently, about eight feet up in a Scotch pine tree. It's happened before - on woodpiles where white-footed mice were living; at bird houses within which white-footed mice also were living; in storage cans filled with sunflower seeds where white-footed mice were eating without permission.

This latest clash was arboreal. It featured me and two white-footed mice who were sleeping.

There I clung, wrapped around a resin-bearing conifer in a jacket too good for the job. Two legs and one hand grasped the Scotch pine trunk. The other hand held a bow saw bent on surgery.

Moving slowly, feeling kinship with three-toed sloths, I

manuevered for position. Above me was six feet of nicely tapered treetop. My task was to sever it without commotion and drag it to the living room, there to adorn it with wooden geese, elves playing tubas and a Holstein cow that always goes on top.

I maneuvered. I steadied myself. I began cutting the four-inch trunk. Because pine is soft and bow saws are sharp, it wasn't a wink before crashdown appeared imminent.

'Wait a minute.'

My better half was calling. She was standing on the ground, pondering marriage to a man who hugs pine trees, when something caught her eye.

'There's a mouse in your tree,' she said. 'See it up there?'

Hold the launch. Send the astronauts home. Mouse in the tree.

The saw blade stopped, a mere slice or two from 'look out below'. Hugging the trunk, with needles poking me from all angles, I tried to look up and see mice. A blop of snow hit me in the face.

'It's right above you, next to that nest.'

There it was, perched on a pine bough near a mass of dried grasses the size of a bowling ball: a tiny rodent, staring down with luminous eyes.

'There's another one,' said ground control. A brown shape, soft as velvet, dashed from the nest and scurried toward the top of the pine.

Great. Just great. In the name of Christmas tree hunting, I was about to ruin a mouse yuletide.

'There's nothing I can do now,' I said. 'I've just about cut through the tree. If I don't finish, it'll blow down with the next strong wind.'

Sad but true. The mice - industrious souls who often maintain more than one nest anyway - would have to move elsewhere.

I shook the trunk a bit, hoping they might run to another tree whose branches intermingled with the one we shared. The mice held their ground and stared, big ears perked forward, whiskers twitching.

A second round of shaking convinced them. Across the branches they ran, one following the other. Safe in a neighboring tree, they dashed down its trunk, across a stretch of frozen ground, and into a snow-covered brush pile.

Smart mice. They must have been using 'Mouse Plan B,' the one that states, 'When primary nest is invaded, fall back immediately to nearby brush pile.'

They'll make out fine, I suspect. White-footed mice eat things like hemlock, birch and maple seeds - food that's available all winter. As for a nest, they can whip one together of milkweed fluff in no time.

As we speak, they're probably cuddled under that brush pile, friends gathered round, recounting the tale of how they met a monster face to face and survived. 'The Sloth and the Bow Saw,' is what they'll call it. It'll be a mouse classic by next year.

WHAT I REALLY WANT FOR CHRISTMAS

What I really want for Christmas is a floating blind that looks like a beaver lodge. It would have inner tubes on the bottom, a plywood floor to sit on and a chicken-wire frame covered with mud and chewed sticks.

It would also have a small hole in the side so my camera could stick out and take pictures of snoozing turtles, courting coots, and muskrats with a lust for cattail tubers.

With my own beaver lodge, I'd be secret king of the swamp. There wouldn't be a heron alive that could tell I was there.

So that's what I want - a beaver lodge - but I'm not sure I'll get one. Santa doesn't relate well to swamps. Ice floes, yes. Tundra, for sure. Swamps they don't have up his way.

To make matters worse, the old boy doesn't work well with chicken wire. It gets caught in his beard.

So I'm preparing myself for disappointment. I'll still wake on Christmas morning, rush downstairs and hope to see a beaver lodge under the tree, but if it isn't there, I'm not going to hold it against some workshop elf who was afraid to try something new.

What I'll do is carry on. I'll give myself a batch of alternative presents to make up for the lost beaver lodge. Memory presents, that's what I'll give; presents I can share.

I'll conjure them up from March through May and November. Then I'll savor them as one savors maple syrup and chopped hickory nuts on vanilla ice cream. After that, I'll pass them along. Hopefully, they'll remind you of outdoor scenes from your own calendar of months gone by. Hopefully, they'll make you anxious for the turning of next year's wheel of seasons.

My gifts to you will be these:

We'll start with a bullfrog on a log, floating through June on a lake with plenty of pickerel weed but no second homes. This will be the friendliest bullfrog you've ever met. It will watch as you paddle closer, tolerate your bumping its log, wait while you load the camera, and pose for close-up after close-up.

You'll also get a year's supply of seashore. I'll give you salt marshes and sea breezes; quohogs on the half shell and seagull footprints at low tide; bays hiding from ocean wind and barrier beaches shifting and sliding as blowing sand sculpts their contours. In the same package you'll find black ducks feeding on mussel beds, sandpipers probing tidal flats, greater scaup barreling low over open water, and crab claws steaming in a big silver pot.

Then I'll give you scenes from the uplands. You'll get flower bouquets: everything from trout stream trillium to cliffside columbine. You'll get birds, too: mourning doves bursting from corn rows, grouse with ruffs puffed, orioles stitching nests that will sway in thunderstorms.

And how about accepting some wood duck babies in hollow trees, or robins on fence posts, or hawks soaring higher, higher, then clean out of sight? Take and enjoy.

Finally, when you think your stocking can't hold any more, I'll stuff in Venus and Mars, what a beautiful sight; horned owls and screech owls and crickets at night; white ash and maple, their fall leaves aflame; chickadees on fingers, with voices quite tame.

And one final gift: the loon's wilderness call. From the great outdoor Santa, Merry Christmas to all!

PART TWO: OTHER PLACES

THE TERMITE VOTE IS KING

SOUTHPORT, NORTH CAROLINA. There comes a point, in the dead of winter, when an unnerving southern wanderlust creeps from Sunday's travel section, whispers of untrammeled beaches and proceeds to shred northern stoicism as a raccoon might dispatch an ear of corn.

Discovering this wanderlust, one must act quickly, lest winter's malaise seep toward other seasons. One must bow to a southern craving. One must breathe an ocean's salt wind, drink the sweet milk of coconuts, and bathe in a hot winter sun.

Most importantly, one must do all these things without care for monetary need.

But how can one fly toward paradise when one's credit card wings have melted in the heat of Christmas expense? It's simple, really. One can fly because one can dream. One can close one's eyes and dream.

There's a sound in the morning, a muffled concussion that rolls over dunes and washes us awake. Waves are breaking just out of sight, sliding toward the beach in precise, foamless curls. Each one's face is lacquered by slanting sun.

The ocean is gentle, still asleep. Beach grass barely twitches; dragonflies buzz above the sand, daring the wind to rise and blow them seaward. The wind will come soon enough. For now it rustles and waits.

We are south, in an ocean place far from the interstate funnel that shunts tourist cars toward Florida motels; in a place where lizards dangle from live oak trees, and vultures soar like funereal kites.

We have found a land where the termite vote swings elections; a land of tobacco sheds and winter crops, where roadside billboards speak of 'Cat-in-the-Bag' Rat Bait, and the Southeastern Swinebreeders Association.

We are south, and the beach wants us walking.

We stroll in the company of ghost crabs who never look away. 'Always face the enemy,' is their battle cry, as they skitter sideways in perpetual pirouette. Their eyes are small black light bulbs; the tips of their claws dance on sand. Exquisitely camouflaged, each crab's carapace looks like beach sand pocked by raindrop craters.

Beyond the breakers, dolphin backs arch in the sunlight. Their dorsal fins slit the surface - black thorns in an ocean garden. Farther offshore, a string of pelicans flaps by in patrol formation. An organized squadron, their heads pointed down to catch the glint of streaking mullet, they show little save wings and pouched beaks.

Running ahead of us at the surf line, wanting to be friends but afraid to ask, are sanderlings. Their legs are a miracle: fragile pins whirring like Olympic walkers at super speed. As a sewing machine stitches fabric, so their bills jab sand in hunting forays.

We approach too closely. The sanderlings erupt in unison, winged sand fleas the wind treats like toys.

Farther down the beach, men and women cast for supper. Rocketing from thick, stubby poles are sinkers that could anchor the QE II. Everyone is using shrimp for bait. Shrimp is cheap here.

Some of the anglers get lucky. A magnificent weakfish is horsed through the shallows and beached with great ballyhoo. Flounder, too, (great, ugly dinner plates) are dredged from the surf and envisioned as fried fillets.

For those who don't catch fish, there is always the salt breeze, a parade of delicate shorebirds, and surf hypnosis to satiate the mind and give pleasure.

The breeze is stiffening. Nimbus giants build in puffy tiers. Perhaps the wind will blow in the late afternoon; a reckless wind that snatches kites from children and twists them around phone wires like broken scarecrows.

Perhaps the wind will blow all night and we can listen. We'll be inside, with the windows open, looking out at the tankers offshore. They are foggy behemoths, looming at the edge of the sea. Their running lights mark the horizon.

TALKING CACTUS SPINES

DEADMAN WASH, ARIZONA. Ed, a bus driver and self-proclaimed tour guide, is driving through the desert talking cactus spines. 'It's the cholla you've got to watch out for,' Ed says, wheeling the bus past saguaro, barrel, prickly pear, and other fleshy statues. 'Some people say a cholla will jump out and grab you.'

Ed is exaggerating, but not by much. Of all the spines on the shimmering flats around us, those of the cholla are most deadly - so deadly, says Ed, that he never drives without packing pliers.

'I had a lady on a tour several weeks ago,' he says. 'We stopped for lunch, and she was backing up to take her friend's picture...'

Smack in an unsuspecting derriere went dozens of cholla spines. Out came Ed's pliers.

'Enjoy yourself out here,' Ed advises a traveler bound for desert wandering, 'but for God's sake don't back up.'

Don't back up. Don't back up. We repeat the words as mantra. A cholla world awaits.

We'll get off Ed's bus and wander the desert for several days. Watching sun rays bake land that hasn't seen rainfall in weeks, we'll come to understand how water gives and takes away; how saving it - soaking it up when it comes - is the key to survival.

Every hour or so, we'll flash back to the jet that brought us here: a pressurized, drink-serving, 600-mph miracle that soared over Louisiana bayous, Mississippi rice fields, and muddy Georgia rivers the color of coffee with cream. There was water everywhere, pristine from blue sky six miles up, endless, bountiful.

It slipped away somewhere near Waco, Texas. It's an Eastern memory now, like humid air, neckties, and lush green woodlands.

What is real in the Arizona desert are landscapes vast and unbroken, treeless vistas accented by rock. Scenery here is Western stereotype: stark in its beauty, majestic but never intimate. Every mesa should have Indians riding across its barren table top. Every gulch should yield cowpokes herding dogies toward watering holes.

Everywhere is adaptation. Plants do it, wildlife does it, people do it, too. Every living thing bends to the contours of life with intense heat. All creatures adjust to unrelenting sun and the precious few raindrops that temper its parching effect.

Saguaro cacti - tall, pleated bandits in pinstripes - play desert blotter when it rains, absorbing water that sustains them during drier times. Barrel cacti are porcupines, their fleshy forms studded with spines to discourage rodents and birds from siphoning moisture. Trees cluster near stream beds that die a bone-dry death in summer but roar with flash floods when rains pound distant slopes.

Avoiding sunlight in the shadow of mesquite and palo verde, desert animals also adapt. The blacktail jackrabbit's ears, with their inordinate surface area, provide ideal ventilation for built-up body heat. Coveys of Gambel's quail scurry through the hottest valleys, nibbling mesquite leaves and cactus fruits, drawing water from them. Rabbit, quail and desert fox rouse at dawn and dusk, when shadows are long and elf owls peer from cactus nest holes.

As for desert people, they offer nightly devotions to the inventor of air conditioning. Anyone doing manual labor in the desert is doing it by 6 A.M. Happy Hour begins in earnest at 4 P.M. There is no daylight savings in Arizona - no one wants the sun staying up longer than it has to. The late news comes on at 10 P.M., so people can go to bed early and beat the sun tomorrow.

When exposure to sunlight is unavoidable, desert inhabitants look to their local newspaper. The front page has a helpful chart showing how long humans can bake in full sun, at different times of the day, before burning.

Another tactic desert people employ to avoid the heat is driving through it at considerable speed. The 55 mph speed limit is a mirage here. Desert interstates tantalize the latent speeder. In perfect condition, without potholes, curves, or obstructions to eternal visibility, they beg you drive faster. After all, aren't the distances great? Isn't the traffic often light or non-existent? There appears no reason, save conservation, to keep the pedal from the floor.

Conservation. Desert people of past generations practiced it because they had to. They needed water, there wasn't much of it, they conserved. Modern desert inhabitants - in numbers far beyond the land's natural ability to sustain them - build dams to create huge lakes, then water lawns with auto-sprinklers that pop up every day.

Thousands of new residents pour into Phoenix each month, lured by warm winters and low humidity. More wells are drilled. More pools are filled. The water table shrinks toward chronic shortage.

'They say, in twenty-five years or so, we're in for real water problems,' says Ed, the bus driver. 'It'll be sooner than that if folks keep moving here.'

Waste not, want not, Ed. It's a creed the jackrabbits have learned to live by.

THE MERMAID AND THE DOLPHIN

MONTAUK, NEW YORK. If you've never been to the ocean, or haven't been recently, we'll go now. Pack a windbreaker, old basketball sneakers, sunglasses, a bird book, and binoculars. Don't pack high-heeled shoes, stock market reports, or clothes that can't come back sprinkled with sand.

Approaching this trip in the proper frame of mind is all-important. Be prepared to get your hair snarled by wind that smells like salt. Be ready to walk on sand decorated with seagull footprint filigree. Prime yourself for a different world, where dunes are mountains and rivers flow with tides.

It is May at the ocean, a time when charter captains

scrape paint and restaurants offer windows on bays without waiting. Fishermen leave in the dark before dawn, returning by sunset with flounder and weakfish. Baymen work shallows for skimmer clams that soon will find chowder. The sea warms imperceptibly, chilling surfers in wetsuits. Life abounds on a margin of sand where earth and water collide.

Beyond the beach are dunes, with cliff-like slopes that face the ocean wind. Their tapered lee sides are covered with mats of tangled shrubs hugging the sand. Bayberry, beach plum, honeysuckle, autumn olive - the wind makes stunted sculptures of them all. With limbs that spread outward (never upward), afraid to lift their heads, they cringe behind the dunes.

Fashioned within their twisted branches are bird hideaways, tunnel cities woven through poison ivy strands. Awash in a fragrance that intoxicates, the cities abound in blooms. Hopping among the blossoms are catbirds, thrashers, redwings, kingbirds, and yellowthroats - upland birds at home within shouting distance of pounding surf. Occasionally, a resident will flit from the tangle, perch on a dead branch, and sing a song that sounds like thorn apple thickets far from the sea.

In a nearby tidal pool stands a snowy egret. Its bill like a spear and body like a statue, the wading bird waits for shimmering silver. As minnows approach, the statue's neck forms a rigid S-curve. As minnows swerve away, the egret loses composure, chasing them with splashing yellow feet.

On the beach nearby, other birds are chasing, birds with legs that blur. They are spotted sandpipers, scouring piles of kelp that storms have ripped from the sea floor and heaped on the beach in twisted piles. The seaweed - a mass of algal ribbons colored red, brown, and green - steams in morning sun. The sandpipers probe and pick, combing filaments for life forms trapped inside.

On rocks just offshore, cormorants dry primitive wings that are waterlogged from fishing forays. Walk too close and the jet-black birds will drop from these rocks like bowling pins, back to an ocean that gives them baby eels and toadfish when they dive.

As an east wind freshens, sand whirlwinds roam the beach. Black-backed gulls cup their wings to hang above the surf. Perhaps a crab will wash ashore, thrown beyond safety by the froth, ripe for picking.

The wind turns up a notch. Eyes water. Legs move forward but are pushed back. Cormorants drop from rocks and bob on whitecaps. Human forms stand battered and exposed, like scarecrows in open fields. The sky beams a brilliant bright blue.

Visitors walk sandy roads to a house nearby, where shingles weather grayish brown and cock pheasants crow in backyard brush. A green-and-white flag flaps on a rusted pole. The green is an ocean background; in white are a mermaid and a leaping dolphin.

Evening is coming and will last forever. Cormorants will fly to the bay side of an oceanic spit, finding refuge in a sheltered cove. Stars will glisten. A mermaid and dolphin will race all night on the wind.

CLOWN ON A WINTER BEACH

MONTAUK, NEW YORK. Summer beach, winter beach. The winds blow differently, the moods are starkly defined.

The summer beach is self-indulgent, covered by human flesh. These folks mean well - kicking balls, cooking sausage, gooping lotion - but always end up scaring the piping plovers, least terns, and other birds that have nested along coastlines for centuries.

Every summer, these birds return to their ancestral nesting grounds and wonder if their grandparents made the wrong choice. Their nest areas are bombarded by errant frisbees; their dignity is assaulted by four-wheel drive vehicles that say 'Ghost Rider' on the side.

Least terns divebomb, scolding. Plovers run for their

lives. They object but are overruled.

The winter beach doesn't have this. It is a cold and windy strand, devoid of terns and self-indulgence. It is left to its own designs, and therein lies its beauty.

Whither the dizzy beachcombers of summers past? Driven to shopping malls by nasty weather. The winter beach breathes easy, rolls free.

There are waves without surfboards, dunes without footprints, stretches of sand without hearts and initials. There are rough, hearty birds bobbing just offshore, keeping warm with down feathers they didn't have to buy.

Three of them come close, diving under breakers, sliding toward shore over each cresting wave. They appear undaunted by the lone man who watches them from the sand, admiring their skill.

They are harlequin ducks, a male and two females. Their ancestors had the right idea about steering clear of crowded beaches.

Greenland, Iceland, the Aleutians - these are summer playgrounds for harlequin ducks, remote places where mountain streams tumble toward beaches no one knows.

Harlequins nest beside these mountain waters. They feed there as well, diving into the strongest currents, propelling themselves to the stream bed with half-closed wings, then walking about on the bottom catching stone fly nymphs.

No one is around to witness this awesome display of animal adaptation. The harlequins like it that way.

Around the middle of November, the streams and rivers in Iceland, Greenland, and the Aleutians become unfriendly for harlequin ducks. The birds are forced to move southward, toward wintering grounds along the coastlines of New England and the Pacific Northwest.

These coasts are deserted when the ducks arrive.

Approaching to within several feet of shore, the harlequins dive beneath waves, prying mollusks from tidal rock. To observe a male harlequin duck bobbing in surf is to watch as beautiful a creature as lives on earth. His body is glossy slate blue. His sides are chestnut. Random white stripes splash here and there on his head.

The drake harlequin dives again. A late afternoon sun gleams on his russet flanks.

The beach is empty.

He's a riotous court jester, but no one watches the show; no one but his attentive female companion, a passing black-backed gull and a silent figure on the beach.

He likes it that way. It's the way it ought to be.

MOB'S MARSH

KEARNY, NEW JERSEY. The police in Kearny are not, by nature, a trusting lot. Perhaps that's because Kearny (pronounced 'Carney'), finds itself located in a less-than-scenic, highly industrialized portion of northern New Jersey where hitchhikers wait weeks at a time for someone to pass by in a trusting frame of mind.

Sandwiched between Newark and Jersey City, only a ten minute drive from Manhattan, the folks in Kearny have learned through countless unfortunate experiences that trusting strangers can be hazardous to one's health. As a consequence, they don't do it much.

Neither do their cops.

Let me say before continuing that I know several policemen and enjoy their company. Becoming intimate with cruising gendarmes, however, is not an avocation.

Why, then, the confrontation with Kearny police? Because the Kearny Marsh has least bitterns.

The police in Kearny know their marsh but not its bitterns. Rather than viewing the blacktop-encircled square mile of fresh water wetland that rests under their jurisdiction as home to an exceptionally elusive wading bird, they see it as an ideal spot for someone to hide Jimmy Hoffa.

Therefore, upon viewing two unknown males lugging a telescope and tripod down the railroad tracks that overlook Kearny Marsh at 9 A.M. on a steaming Sunday morning in early August, what choice does a patrolling policeman have but to investigate?

'*Bweeeep!*' A whistle of uncanny piercing ability erupts from the marsh's periphery. The birders freeze, transfixed. What bird? What unknown, awesome call?

Actually, it is not a bird calling. It is an automobile: a blue and white one with a red glass bubble on top. Idling on the dead-end road where we have just parked, its occupant is about to speak to us through a large electric bullhorn affixed to the auto's exterior.

'Come down to the car,' blasts the bullhorn.

He wants us to come down to the car. He wants to talk about Jimmy Hoffa.

Getting into civil conversation range is easier said than done. Between us and the cop lies a mountainous heap of half-burned automobile tires that would intimidate Parris Island marines.

Carefully - with telescope, field guides, and binoculars prominently displayed - we scale the rubberized burial mound, descend its blackened backside and approach the police car.

'What are you guys up to?'

'We're watching birds.'

There is a momentary silence as our interrogator chews on the filter of an unlit cigarette.

'Is that OK?' we query, in tones that exude cooperative spirit.

'Yes and no,' replies the gendarme, pausing again to watch us perspire. 'It's OK as long as you don't stray too far. We had a guy break down out here a week ago, and when he got back from phoning for help, his car was gone.'

Hmmmmmm.

'Just keep an eye out,' adds our protector, before heading off in search of more meaningful encounters.

It's not often one is allowed the thrill of birding under threat of car theft. We decided to chance it, and spent the next hour keeping one eye on common gallinules and the other on a Honda stickshift.

We saw coots, coots, and more coots - paddling through the duckweed with an impressive output of fuzzy, orange-headed chicks. We saw common egrets and snowy egrets, waiting, stonelike, for a fish or amphibian to wander into spearing range.

We saw a least bittern.

Skulking, furtive, only twelve inches tall, least bitterns are camera shy. Uncomfortable in open places, they prefer wandering about in reed beds, there to climb on cattail stems with the agility of island boys on coconut palms.

Thus it was with great excitement that we watched one such recluse rise from a cattail clump, flap awkwardly across the marsh for fifty yards or so, and plop down unceremoniously in another cattail clump.

'Have you ever seen a least bittern?' asked my companion.

'I'm not sure,' I replied.

'You have now,' he said, and we headed back to the car.

Somewhere within the whirlpool that sucked us back toward Manhattan, I pondered Kearny Marsh and said, 'You know, it really wouldn't be a bad place to hide Jimmy Hoffa.'

'Some say that's right where he is,' my friend replied.

PART THREE: OTHER FRIENDS

FAMILY SCANDAL

No one ever accused the house wren of being a master of understatement. When something bothers this half-pint songbird, it erupts with peeved admonitions.

So it was on a mid-June morning, as we peered into the wren's tangled domain to see what all the fuss was about. The shubbery buzzed with scolding sounds. Wrens flitted from branch to branch, their tails erect and danders aroused. Wren youngsters must have just left the nest, we figured. Parent wrens were protecting their charges and discouraging intruders.

We were right - almost. The doting parents had a newly fledged youngster, all right, but it wasn't a wren. Perched haughtily on an overhanging branch, absorbing all their attention, sat a spoiled-rotten, hog-it-all, lummox of a baby cowbird.

Why, you ask, should a pair of wrens give a hoot about the welfare of a baby cowbird, let alone care for it as one of their own? Because they have been victimized by one of nature's oldest con games, a scheme that has turned them into unwilling foster patents while the shell game's perpetrators are free to carouse without care.

Here's how the scam works:

Winter turns to spring. Male and female cowbird meet and mate. Female cowbird sneaks into wren's nest and lays a single egg. Wrens raise baby cowbird, get stuck with a bossy freeloader. Adult cowbirds go on vacation.

To more thoroughly understand this complex tale of parasitism, we must go back to its roots, on the plains of primeval North America.

Even then, brown-headed cowbirds shied from traditional family life. They lead nomadic lives, too busy to settle down. When the great bison herds grazed midwestern plains from horizon to endless horizon, cowbirds always went with them, trailing in their dusty wake. The buffalo kicked up insects; the cowbirds dined well. Keeping up with their nomadic benefactors assured the cowbirds a constant food supply.

A major problem inherent in keeping up involved finding several weeks in which to raise young. By the time a pair of cowbirds had built a nest, incubated eggs, and nurtured helpless nestlings to the fledgling stage, their meal ticket on the hoof usually had moseyed over a distant horizon and disappeared.

Generations of cowbirds undoubtedly learned the hard way. Those that dallied in favor of domesticity ran the risk of death by starvation. Those that gave up family life

to keep tabs on where the buffalo roamed became vaga-
bond disciples of gradual population decline and eventual
extinction.

What the cowbirds needed was a liberated lifestyle that
would allow them to stay with the herd while maintaining
species continuity. They found it in parasitism. They
would lay their eggs in other birds' nests, catch the buffalo express on its way out of town, and let someone else
worry about feeding their young.

Even though the bison herds are gone, and cowbirds
have expanded their range to cover most of the eastern
United States, the winged hobos have not abandoned
their parasitic lifestyle. Finding over 200 bird species as
suitable hosts, they continue to lead the good life at someone else's expense.

Certain species, such as robins, bluejays, and catbirds,
react strongly to discovering a strange egg in their nests.
They will puncture it and toss it out. Others, such as the
yellow warbler, build a new nest on top of the cowbird
egg and start over. The yellow-breasted chat will abandon
its nest completely if it is visited by a cowbird.

For the most part, however, unwitting parents care
dutifully for a foster child that represents almost certain
death for their rightful brood.

Compared to those laid by its host, a cowbird's egg is
almost always larger. Because of its size, it receives more
warmth from the incubating female and hatches first. By
the time its nestmates have emerged, the cowbird
transplant is clamoring for attention and gobbling up
every morsel the parent birds can bring back to the nest.
Newly hatched red-eyed vireos, song sparrows, and
house wrens remain weak and stunted. They die in the
nest or are pushed out by the ravenous intruder.

Of small consolation to parents that end up raising a
stranger is the fact that cowbirds are careful not to cause
a decline in the numbers of their host species. That would

be killing the goose that laid the golden eggs. Without hosts there would be no nests to invade. Cowbirds usually victimize common species that can stand the strain of lost young.

As soon as a cowbird can fly, it leaves its guardians and seeks its own kind. By September, huge cowbird flocks have convened for southern migration flights.

With spring's arrival, the cowbirds return to familiar fields of their youth. There males woo female counterparts with a no-nonsense pitch reminiscent of a come-on in the classifieds: *Wanted. Companion for happy-go-lucky affair. No strings attached. Must enjoy travel. No children, please.*

ON HUMMINGBIRD ADDICTION

Anyone who can watch a ruby-throated hummingbird at close range without becoming enthralled must have dead batteries. Those blurring wings, that needle-shaped bill on a body so small - everything about this bird is extraordinary. Its vital statistics are a stream of superlatives.

This was the first year hummingbirds deemed my yard worth visiting. Their change of heart was due to my wife, who planted bright red clumps of a perennial called bergamot, or bee balm. I also helped out when I put up a hummingbird feeder.

Hummingbird feeders are clear glass cylindars filled with artificial nectar. Hummingbirds can sit on perches at the bottom of the cylindars and draw nectar from them via tubes that are surrounded by red plastic flowers.

Call it a weakness, but hummingbirds are pushovers for bright colors. They see those plastic flowers and can't resist. They come buzzing into your life, and you watch, amazed.

What you see is a bird of extremes. Hummingbirds are extremely small, extremely fast, extremely agile. The whirring of their wings - loud at close range, like a giant wasp - can startle you if you're outside reading the paper, your head is two feet from the hummingbird feeder, and they suddenly show up for supper.

If you turn too fast, they're gone, buzzing into a nearby woodland with incredible quickness. If you turn very slowly, you can watch metabolic wonders at work.

A female approaches, resembling a giant bumblebee as she zips across the yard at 30 mile per hour. One foot from the feeder she stops on a dime, hovers for a moment with tail pumping and wings a blur, then lands on a perch with feet so small they can barely walk on land. Iridescent green on the back, with white undersides, she is three inches long from tip of beak to stubby tail.

Dip ...dip ...dip. Her brush-like tongue laps nectar from a plastic flower. Somewhere nearby are young hummingbirds that may taste the sweetness second hand. Dip ...dip ...dip. The female will mix this nectar with insects or spiders and stuff the resulting concoction down nestling throats. She'll do this for three weeks, without help from her mate, until the young have fledged from a nest no bigger than half a walnut shell.

The male appears, his scarlet throat patch the size of a garden pea. The female whirs from her perch; the male chases her, chattering in high-pitched squeaks. For him, late summer offers few other diversions. His parental duties ended with conception. He has no idea where his offspring are or how they're doing. He has never seen the nest his mate constructed of lichens and plant fibers, then strengthened with spider silk.

He is free to perch on the garden fence, feeding only himself.

He sits and I watch, thinking of all the things humming-birds are famous for. Did you know the hummingbird has the shortest small intestine of all birds? It's two inches long. Did you know its wings beat 75 times a second, its heart pounds 615 times per minute, it can fly backwards and has 1,500 feathers if you count them on an average summer day?

Were you aware that hummingbirds are solitary migrants, crossing the Gulf of Mexico by themselves, usually low over the waves, on their way to wintering grounds in Central America? Did you have any idea their breast muscles are larger, in proportion to body size, than any bird on earth? Or, that their hearts, also propor-tionately larger than any other species, comprise 20 per-cent of their total body weight?

You probably didn't; that's a lot to know about hum-mingbirds unless you're hooked on them. Of course, if you had a clump of bee balm around the house, you couldn't help but get hooked. Hummingbirds demand it of those who watch them. They are, as I said, irresistible, tiny intestines and all.

NOT A BAD EGG IN THE LOT

Whenever I get depressed about human beings, I think about chickadees. They make for a better night's sleep.

Chickadees, for example, don't know a thing about nuclear bombs. They've never heard of them. In addition, chickadees never hold up banks, wear loud, flashy clothes or try to impress other chickadees with how smart they are.

Chickadees are spirited but not overly aggressive, inquisitive without being nosy, trusting but never gullible.

And you know the best thing of all about chickadees? Every one is like this, to the bird. You don't have to put out ads begging for a few good chickadees; they're all good. There's not a bad egg in the lot.

The same, however, cannot be said for the two-legged videophiles upon whom they are forced to depend for planetary stewardship.

Now you may think I'm being overly harsh here; too tough on humans, too soft on chickadees. You probably think there are at least one or two greedy, self-destructive chickadees living around the block or in the next town. There aren't. I checked it out.

For twelve months, beginning in August 1982, I rated the personality of every human being and every chickadee I met on an evaluation form. In the case of humans, I rated only those to whom I had been formally introduced during the period. As for chickadees, only individuals I was able to observe through binoculars for a minimum of five minutes were included.

You're familiar with the kind of form I used. It's like those you see at work, where humans are given number ratings to indicate their suitability as keepers of the corporate faith. The forms usually rate employees from 1 to 5, with 5 being 'clearly outstanding.' Unfortunately, there's never a clearly outstanding person around the office. No one ever gets a 5.

I decided to use the 1-to-5 method on my form, too, but vowed to look extra hard for outstanding humans. I did, and found some, but they still took it on the chin when compared with chickadees.

The results make this clear.

Of the 173 human beings I met for the first time in 1982, only 23 rated a 5. Foremost in my mind are a young man who stopped the buzzing noise in my car stereo and a lady at the grocery check-out who double-bagged my dog food cans.

Twenty-three outstanding humans out of 173: that's really not too bad. And there were a good many 4-rated people in the bunch as well. But chickadees put them to shame. Of the 68 I watched, every one got a 5 rating.

Imagine: 68 chickadees and not one clunker. Every one

could dance like a gymnast on bare winter branches; every one waited patiently while house finches hogged bird feeder space; every one was energetic, with fire in its eye.

Every one took a gloomy day and made it bright.

If you find a human being with all these qualities, tackle said person at once. It may be the last one you'll see for some time.

If you find such a chickadee, you've just found an average Joe.

PITY THE POOR OPOSSUM?

The opossum, poor soul, is not very smart.

Squat and slow, he scuttles across the nation's highways with suicidal resolve. Refusing to store food for winter, he scrounges about the neighborhood like a wayward beggar, wandering a frozen world with naked, frost-prone ears.

It's a tough life for the poor, stupid opossum. Out to lunch when nature gave out good looks and intelligence, he is doomed by his shortcomings, fated for extinction in a world where brains and good looks get ahead.

Go tell that to opossums. They'll laugh in your face. They'll laugh as they expand their range northward. They'll laugh as they continue making babies by the bucketful. They'll laugh as they plod through life with the same dull persistence that has characterized them for millennia.

You don't talk extinction to opossoms; you talk success.

But how can a dimwit like the opossum succeed? Doesn't survival of the fittest mean survival of the smartest? Not in the case of opossums. If nature gave out grades for intelligence, they would have failed out long ago. Instead, nature rewards adaptability. Here opossums move to the head of the class.

An excellent example would be the opossum's tolerance of varied climatic conditions. At the turn of the century there was no such thing as a northeastern opossum. The rat-tailed marsupials were restricted to southern states where warm temperatures reminded them of their ancestral homes in Central and South America.

When their southern range became overcrowded, and den site demand began exceeding supply, a few daring opossum pioneers set out for greener, albeit colder, pastures. They've been pushing northward ever since, now occupying all the Northeast except northernmost New England.

Another example of adaptability is the opossum's philosophy on dining. This 6- to 10-pound scavenger is agreeable to a fault about its dinner fare. The trick is finding something it won't consume. No road-kill is too rank; no bird's egg too rotten. Fruits, nuts, small mammals, worms, insects, garbage - all are fallen upon as choice morsels.

In addition, opossums are not fussy about accommodations. They will live happily in deserted woodchuck burrows and squirrel nests, hollow trees, brush piles and culverts. They will even live under your back porch, if you make a little hole for them to get in and out.

With such an adaptable personality, is it any wonder the plodding opossum has become an evolutionary success?

Adaptability, however, is not the only trait responsible

for this century's startling opossum explosion. As mentioned earlier, opossums make lots of little opossums. Nature smiles on fecundity.

California condors produce one offspring every two years. They're all but gone from the wild. Opossums can bear two litters of 13 young in one year. They face no such problem.

Finally, opossums have succeeded because of efficient design. Fossil records indicate they have changed little since appearing on earth some 90 million years ago. So what if they waddle, are near-sighted and have pointy faces? It's the total package that counts. The opossum's is a proven winner.

Edsels may come and Edsels may go. Opossums are here to stay.

OCEAN SUBSTITUTE

Living hours from the ocean, unable to sniff a salt breeze with anything approaching regularity, I have taken to embracing substitutes.

A knobbed whelk shell sits on the mantel. It gets clamped on a left ear, then a right ear, every other Friday so I can hear wind skimming tops off incoming breakers.

There is an ocean cobblestone from my favorite rocky beach. An officially designated pet rock, it rests atop the radio, reminding me of waves that grind sharp edges toward ovate smoothness. I hold it periodically, marveling at the power of repetition.

There are killdeer flying overhead, calling. If the truth be known, killdeer are the best ocean substitutes of all. Not only do they look like shorebirds, they act like shorebirds. Officially speaking, they are shorebirds, but they shun the seaside for inland climes.

These most widely distributed and best known of all North American shorebirds prefer meadows and pastures, mud banks and gravel roofs, often far from saltwater sounds. There's only one explanation for this oceanic aversion: killdeer were placed on earth to make inland ocean lovers feel less deprived. Their mission is to allow Kansans, Nebraskans and others far from the sea an opportunity to sense the ebb and flow of tidal pools.

Breeding throughout southern and central Canada, and most of the United States, killdeer look most like shorebirds when they run. Scampering over cultivated fields on stiff, whirring toothpicks, then stopping suddenly to spear a beetle or grasshopper, they constitute perfect upland copies of their ocean cousins, the Wilson's and piping plovers, that scamper on sandy spits.

Killdeer also show shorebird tendencies in building their 'nests,' those minimal depressions on bare ground, lined with a pebble or two, that serve as home for three to five splotchy eggs and a pair of nervous parents.

Other shorebirds, including sandpipers that breed on treeless tundra flats, show a similar fancy for bare-bones decor. They also produce beautifully camouflaged eggs, as killdeer do, and chicks that run from the nest within minutes of hatching.

Indeed, killdeer and their shorebird kin share much in common. When it comes to pleasing landlocked birders, however, there's no comparison.

Take a dreary March day, when migrating killdeer make winter-weary souls look ahead to April sunshine. As they beat overhead on erratic wings, dashing this way and that, their strident *kill-dee, kill-dee* offers a spring promise as uplifting as the bluebird's warbled whistle.

Then there are June afternoons - the kind that roll toward sunset on puffy, cumulous wheels - when nesting killdeer turn rock-strewn fields into summer stages.

Rushing from their nests when danger approaches, the parents flounder in the dirt, drooping their wings and dragging their tails. 'We are injured, easy prey,' is the message. 'Follow us and eat well tonight.'

The predator that follows is led away from killdeer eggs and toward a classic ruse. At a safe distance from the nest, the wounded parent miraculously recovers and flies away. The cat, or coyote, or hapless human is left to wonder what went wrong.

Finally, there are moonlit nights in mid-July; nights when the cry of a killdeer rouses those who toss on summer sheets and try to dream.

Why do you call at night, mysterious shorebird? Are you filled with ancestral yearning? Do you miss the ocean? Shall I take you there?